Ahead Danger

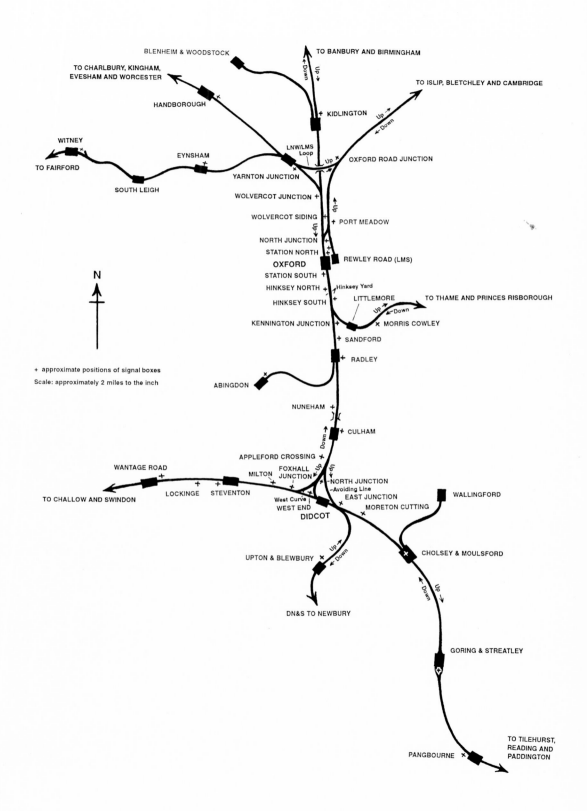

Ahead Danger
and other tales of Didcot Railwaymen

Collected by Patrick Kelly
Edited by Will Adams

Silver Link Publishing Ltd

First published in 2019

British Library Cataloguing in Publication Data

A catalogue record for this book is available from the British Library.

ISBN 978 1 85794 535 5

Silver Link Publishing Ltd
The Trundle
Ringstead Road
Great Addington
Kettering
Northants NN14 4BW

Tel/Fax: 01536 330588
email: sales@nostalgiacollection.com
Website: www.nostalgiacollection.com

Printed and bound in the Czech Republic

Contents

Preface

I have written this book so that all the ex-railwaymen could have their stories read by people 'from the other side of the tracks', giving them an insight into the everyday workings of British Railways, including during the war years. I also recall some of my work colleagues, and the various heavy and dirty jobs we had to undertake at Didcot shed.

The book includes details about the Membury family, all railway signalmen, with pictures from Ken Membury, the last of the line. Eric, one of four sons, was involved in the accident at Appleford Crossing on the night of 12/13 November 1942. The signalman at Appleford was Jack Gough, and the only known picture of the incident is included here. The unlucky engine crew were Driver Forbe and Fireman Jarvis, both from Didcot. The book concludes with another strangely similar accident at the same spot just 10 years later.

Reading shed is also brought into the picture, with the memories of John McNamara and Derek Dawson. The marshalling yard there is also featured, with pictures of USA engines working there as part of the wartime Lend-Lease programme, having arrived by sea at Southampton and Cardiff.

Also described is the Polar Star enginemen's hostel at Didcot, the scene of a variety of humorous goings-on!

Pat Kelly
Norfolk, 2019

Acknowledgements

I would like to thank all my ex-railwaymen friends, their sons, daughters and families, for their help with this book, in particular: Eileen and Ken Membury; Marcella Irving, daughter of ex-railwayman Eric Membury; John Pritchard, ex-railwayman; Charlie Caulkett, ex-railwayman; Bill Morris, Steventon station, son of an ex-railwayman; Archie Davies's long-lost son; Derek Everson, ex-railwayman; Laurence Waters, Great Western Trust;

John McNamara, ex-railwayman; John Law; Science & Society Picture Library, London; Peter Sedge; R. J. Russell, ex-railwayman, for his knowledge of items in this book; Frank Dumbleton; Allan Brown, ex-railwayman; Cyril Tolley, ex-railwayman, gone but not forgotten; Lewis Beadle; W. Turner; Derek Dawson, ex-railwayman; and Mr Chris Gasson for the stories of his late father, author Harold Gasson.

An early postcard view of Loudwater station, south of High Wycombe on the branch from Maidenhead. *John Law collection*

Chapter 1
Ahead Danger: 13 November 1942

The Membury family

The small picturesque station at Loudwater in Buckinghamshire was on the 2 miles 29 chains branch line to High Wycombe from Maidenhead on the former Great Western main line. The station was located at the bottom of Treadaway Hill and served both Loudwater and Flackwell Heath. Opening in 1854, it became a halt in 1968 with the decreasing service on the line. The station was closed and demolished in 1970. It was a pretty station with a garden kept by the British Railways staff, growing flowers and shrubs.

Eric Membury in the signal box at Loudwater. *Marcella Irving collection*

Another view of the interior of the signal box. *Marcella Irving collection*

Eric Membury was the signalman there, a second-generation railwayman. His father was Frank William Membury, born on 24 July 1879 at Oxford. He worked as a signalman at Kineton, Chipping Campden, Yarnton and Didcot East Junction. His granddaughter Marcella recalls that Frank courted and married Miss Lavinia Octavia Walton, born on 10 December 1874, from Kineton. They married at Chipping Campden on 21 May 1898. Lavinia was in service and a very hard woman, says Marcella, 'but I guess she had to be with four sons and two daughters. I seem to remember a lovely picture of my grandmother – she was quite a looker and five years older than grandad.'

Frank and Lavinia's first son was Francis William, born on 19 July 1899. He started

Frank and Lavinia Membury. *Marcella Irving collection*

work in 1914 at Kintbury, near Newbury in West Berkshire, then worked at Chipping Camden, Greenford, Haddenham in Buckinghamshire on the GWR&LNER joint line, Oxford North, Oxford North Junction (the link to the LMS), Oxford Station South in 1944, Wheatley in 1954, then Thame and Princes Risborough at the time of the Beeching cuts. He then worked at the Morris Cowley car works of BL until he retired in 1964. Francis had one son, Ken, who was

Right: Councillor Edgar Smewin, Mayor of Oxford, is supervised by Signalman Francis Membury in Oxford South signal box on 10 November 1947.

Below: Francis Membury exchanges the single line token at Wheatley signal box, between Oxford and Princes Risborough.

B.R. 14301/517

G. A. V. PHILLIPS
Divisional Traffic *Manager*
C. F. E. HARVEY
Assistant Divisional Traffic *Manager*

Telephone
PADDINGTON 7000
Ext. **2776.**
Telegraphic Address
TRAFMAN WESRAIL
LONDON T&SN
Telex No. 24126

WESTERN REGION
OF
BRITISH RAILWAYS
DIVISIONAL TRAFFIC MANAGER
(LONDON DIVISION)
PADDINGTON STATION
LONDON, W.2

Your Reference

Our Reference IR/18347/3.

9th July, 1964.

Dear Mr. Membury,

    I am sorry the time has arrived for you to conclude your active association with the Railway.

    Your retirement on 26th July will bring to a close more than 50 years' unblemished service of which you may be justly proud. I should, therefore, like to take this opportunity of thanking you, both officially and on my own behalf, for the valued services you have rendered throughout your long career.

    I have pleasure in enclosing a congratulatory message from the General Manager and Mr. Phillips.

    Please accept my best wishes for your future well-being in the leisure of retirement.

Yours sincerely,

For G. A. V. PHILLIPS.
J. W. Loder
Divisional Movements Manager

WHEATLEY.

W E S T E R N

Francis Membury

THIS CERTIFICATE records that on the occasion of your retirement the Western Railway Board and Management desire to congratulate you upon the completion of **50** years' employment, and wish you health and happiness in your retirement.

They also wish to place on record their high appreciation of the service which you have rendered to the railways and to the public during that period.

F. Phillips
Divisional Manager

26th July, 1964.

C. A. Firres
General Manager

R A I L W A Y   B O A R D

Above and left: Francis Membury leaves the railway.

Above: Tony Membury.

Right: Bill Membury, shunter and foreman at Moreton Cutting.

born on 31 January 1934.

    Frank's second son was Alec, born in 1902; he worked at Ashendon Junction on the GWR&LNER joint line, and North Moreton Cutting. Alec had four sons: William, a shunter and Foreman at Moreton Cutting; Stanley, who joined the Navy during the Second World War and emigrated to Australia; Joe, a goods guard, shunter and signalman at Appleford; and Tony, a foreman and driver at Didcot shed, a driver at Old Oak Common and a member of the 6024 Preservation Society.

    Tony started work at 14½ years old at Didcot shed, and during his working life he had plenty of experience on the footplate working 'Kings' to Wolverhampton and the West Country. With all that knowledge and experience he had wonderful memories of his railway life. He retired from Old Oak Common depot as a driver in 1994 and to mark the occasion the support crew on preserved 'King' No 6024 gave up their footplate turns on a return journey from Stratford-upon-Avon to Didcot so that Tony could join the crew.

Needless to say, Tony assumed control and no one who was on that run will ever forget the excellent running that delivered the passengers back to Didcot 20 minutes early. This was the first time he had witnessed passengers gathering around the engine cab and bursting into applause. Tony married Margaret and had two sons.

Son number three, Alan, was born in 1903, and was a boilersmith at Didcot shed. He had one son, Victor.

Finally came Eric in 1904. He was signalman at Loudwater, and later Didcot North Junction. He had two daughters, June and Marcella. He was christened Greville Eric Membury, but was always known by his second name. As soon as he was old enough he started on the railway working at Loudwater. However, he wanted to get back to Didcot after a long spell working at Loudwater signal box, with nothing very interesting happening, the same routine, day in, day out. It was single-line working, and he had to operate the capstan level crossing gate wheel. Boredom was setting in at a very early age. But he was gaining more experience every day.

Eventually an opportunity arose for this young man; looking at the notice board in the Station master's office, scouring the list of vacancies, with great joy he suddenly found that a signalman was required to work in a Class 1 box at Didcot. Thus Eric become a signalman at North Junction.

After courting he married a lady from High Wycombe, but was very happy to get back to Didcot. Marcella remembers, 'Dad was so pleased to be back with all his friends but my Mum preferred to stay in High Wycombe than Didcot, which was too close to the in-laws! But he was dedicated to his family and the Great Western Railway!'

Marcella recalls that her mother was seriously ill in 1960 and was in hospital for a few months. 'I stayed with my Dad but he had to work shifts including nights, and I was often left alone in the house. His

colleague from Appleford box had sadly taken his own life recently and I remember my Dad being quite upset about this. One day I woke at around 8.00am and the house was empty – my Dad had not come home. All sorts of awful thoughts went through my mind and I raced to the station. Can you picture a skinny, much distressed teenager, 15 years old, ploughing through the queue of commuters at Didcot waiting to get their tickets, and demanding to know where my Dad was! He was such a good Dad and so reliable – it really had me worried, but all was well. They were able to put me through to Dad, who had stayed on in North Junction signal box as his colleague had been waylaid and was 2 hours late for his shift. So all ended well, and the ticket staff (and the queue of people!) were so kind, and Dad was soon back, having had to cycle from work. I'm not sure who the colleague was, but Dad really liked him, but said that he was often a little late! But no way could Dad have left the box unmanned.'

Eric Membury liked to play little jokes while working at North Junction signal box. 'One day,' remembers Marcella, 'he somehow tied a rope behind him and then made it look like he was hanging – someone took a photo. He was always getting up to pranks like this. He had an incredible sense of humour and was a great Dad.'

Eric Membury playing around, 'hanging' at North Junction signal box.

Reading relief

On goods trains coming down from London, a Reading relief engine crew took over from the Old Oak Common crew at Reading West Junction. The following describes a typical sequence of events as might have happened on the night of 12 November 1942. The engine was 2-8-0 No 2899, and the London men passed on their observations about the mixed goods train and their journey from Old Oak Common.

Now the Reading men had a journey down to Didcot where they would need water for the tender, as Goring water troughs were low. They made Didcot with not much water in the tender; at the water column the canvas bag was put into the tender's filler hole while the Reading driver operated the valve until the fireman shouted to shut it as the tender was overflowing onto Platform 5, being filled beyond its capacity of 3,500 gallons.

Noticing that the engine was at the water column being filled, the Reading guard walked down to the end of the freight train taking notes of events or anything that might have happened on the journey; he would keep an eye on any item arising and report it to the next guard when they reached Challow and the Swindon relief crew.

The Reading fireman went to the outside water tap and filled the billycans to the top with cool clear water, placing them on the firebox shelf where they would get hot so they could have a brew later. Meanwhile the Didcot Carriage & Wagon 'wheel-tapper' was walking up the freight train tapping the wheels with his small long-handled hammer. Before they could move on to their next stop the Inspector had to check the axle boxes for hot bearings, leaving the lids open for his mate, walking with him and carrying a bucket of grease and an oilcan, to replenish the axle boxes, being allowed 30 minutes to do so while the train was standing.

The Inspectors were dedicated to their work, checking both goods trains and passenger coach axle boxes in the vicinity at

any time of day or night. If a wagon or coach had a 'hot box' they would get the vehicle off the train and shunt it into the yard. It was the same with coach wheels; if there was a dead sound from the wheel, the coach came off the passenger train, was shunted into the yard and replaced.

The signalman wanted the goods train cleared away, and it was 'given the board' to move off. The C&W Inspector gave the OK to the guard that all was correct. The fireman was told to give two blasts on the Great Western whistle. He looked out of the side window through a crack in the 'Zeppelin sheet' and waved to the guard, who waved back with a white lamp, and the train started to pull away slowly. The driver asked the fireman to pull the sand lever to allow sand to run onto the slippery rail to stop the four pairs of 4ft 7½in driving wheels from slipping and to give a better grip with the weight of the goods train behind them, as the regulator was opened up to the first notch. A wave to the signalman, and they pulled away along the Down Relief line.

The mixed train was comprised of loose-coupled goods wagons, and the next stop was Challow station, the western boundary of the London Division. There the Reading men would take over an eastbound goods train heading for the 'Gully' at the West Curve, Didcot. As No 2899 started to pull away the driver opened the regulator to the next notch. The wagons started to shake and rattle as speed increased. The fireman removed the long bar poker from the tender and, with his gloves on, poked the fire to get rid of the clinker that held the fire to the grate; he then started to shovel coal into the firebox, placing it on either side, and put on the blower to draw the fire. When he replaced the poker in its slot at the side of the tender it was glowing white hot and smoking from the heat in the firebox.

Between bouts of firing he considered how to keep on top of the fire and maintain steam pressure, keeping an eye on the black needle of the steam gauge at 225lb per square inch; in order for the driver to be able to keep the speed up the fire had to be just right and white hot, making sufficient steam to keep the goods train moving on to their next stop. Firemen were praised in Great Western sheds for their ways of working, and for being tidy on the footplate. Next he opened up the air flow, with the blower still on, until the fire was burned off, then he shut the blower. His next job was to put water in the boiler as the steam pressure started to rise. He opened the valve above the boiler to allow the water to be pumped into it and bring the steam pressure down slowly, checking the sight gauge glass until he saw the water bobbing up and down at a good level.

The fireman now had a general clean-up as the footplate was in a terrible state; he wanted to clean the area of coal dust, so washed down the wooden floor with the prep pipe. Steam started to rise from the floorboards from the heat of the fire glowing behind the iron firedoors; he opened them a crack to peer in, saying to himself quietly, 'Good level.'

Sitting down on his wooden seat, he looked up and saw the 'Zeppelin sheet' blowing in the wind, so he tightened up the springs that held it in place and checked the side blackout covering sheets that stopped the glow escaping from the firebox; they were are at war and did not want to show enemy planes in the sky a red glow coming from the engine as it sped along. This reminded him to check where he had put his tin helmet and gas mask in case they were needed urgently; both were together on the hook near the quarter-light window with the driver's set.

Description of Block Signalling on Principal Running Lines (Dots indicate Block Posts)	Stations, Signal Boxes, etc.	Mileage		Running Lines			Loops and Refuge Sidings		Permanent Speed restrictions miles per hour		Runaway Catch Points (Spring or Unworked Trailing Points)		Gradient (Rising unless otherwise shown) 1 in	Remarks
		M.	Ch.	Additional Up	Principal	Additional Down	Description	Standage Wagons L. & V.	Down	Up	Line	Position		
	PADDINGTON TO CHALLOW—*contd.*													
	Goring and Streatley	44	60											
	Cholsey & Moulsford (See Table "C2" for Wallingford Branch)	48	37				URS	68	10			Through Junction Up Relief line to Wallingford Branch		
	Moreton Cutting	51	29						40	40		Down Relief line to Down Main line / Up Main line to Up Relief line		
	Didcot East (See page 33 for Didcot Avoiding Loop)	{51 / 52	74 / 38						70			Down Main line to Down Relief line		
										70		Up Relief line to Up Main line		
										70		Through Junction Down Relief line to Up Relief line and to Down Avoiding Loop		
	Signal R 217								25	25		Up Relief line to No. 5 Platform line and vice versa		
	Didcot Signal R 176 (See page 24 for Oxford line)	53	10						15			Through Junction Down Relief line to Oxford line		
	Signal R 276								15 / 15			Through Junction Up Relief line to Oxford line / Up Relief line to Down Relief line		
	Signal R 278								15			No. 5 Platform line to Oxford line		
	Foxhall Junction (See page 34 for Didcot West Curve line)	53	55						25 / 25	25 / 25		Down Relief line to Down Main line / Up Goods line to C.E.G.B. Sidings / Up Main line to Up Relief line / Up Relief line to West Curve		
	Signal R 84								25			Down Main line to Down Goods line and over Goods line		
	Signal R 286													

Details of the route from Paddington to Challow, as described in the Sectional Appendix to the Working Timetable in 1975. *Cyril Tolley collection*

Looking out, the fireman saw that Steventon station was in sight so it wasn't far now as they steamed along the road. As they passed beneath the road bridge they heard the blast from the chimney banging out the rhythm of the pistons pounding in the cylinders, powering the heavy goods train into the dark of the peaceful night. They had now reached Steventon station and the fireman looked out through the tarpaulin

Steventon interlude

Right: George Hickman was born in 1878, and is maybe 25 to 30 years old when seen here at Burghclere station near Newbury. *Bill Morris collection*

Below: George Hickman at Steventon signal box. *George Hickman*

Below: Station Master Mr Greenman, Jimmy Greenaway, Dick Greenaway (his son), Charlie Chapman and Arnold Mace at Steventon in 1930. *Bill Morris collection*

into the sky for any enemy planes that might be following the train on its journey towards Swindon and its marshalling yard; a

loose bomb along the route could do a lot of damage.

As No 2899 approached the outskirts

Above: Station Master Mr Greenman looks out from the signal box with Jimmy Greenaway, while on the ground are (left to right) Charlie Chapman, Dick Greenaway and Arnold Mace. *Bill Morris collection*

Below: Steventon station, 1950s. One of the station seats is now in Albert Park in Abingdon, donated by

Tony Chappell's daughter. Her brother, also named Tony, was a keen trainspotter and when Steventon station closed on 7 December 1964 he bought the bench and some other British Railways equipment, including a fire bucket. When his son left home, Tony senior donated the bench to Christ's Hospital, a local charity that runs the park and almshouses.

A Class 'H' mixed goods trains (signalled as '1 pause 4' on the telegraph block instruments between signal boxes) runs through Steventon station. It is carrying one lamp above the smokebox door and another above the centre of the buffer beam. *W. Turner, Great Western Trust collection*

of Challow they could see the smokebox door of the train they were to relieve, the 2.30pm freight from Swindon to Bordesley, Birmingham District, shining in the dark. (All the station nameplates were removed during the war because spies might have passed on information to the enemy!) The Swindon locomen were waiting with their train on the up line at the end of the station. The Reading driver slowly applied the vacuum brake to slow the engine and, with the crash of buffers from the mixed goods train coming together, they came to a stop.

Gathering their satchels, helmets and gas masks with the empty billycans and the spare shovel, the Reading crew started their walk to the waiting engine across the wooden sleeper crossing between the platforms. They waited for their guard, who was on his way to meet them, so they could cross over together; all three then walked across the sleepers and up to the station at the side of the tracks for safety.

By the time they approached the engine it was 10.30pm, and they saw the blackout coverings around the footplate and over the cab roof to contain the glare from the firebox. The driver and his fireman explained to the Swindon relief crew that they had had a good trip from Reading, there were no faults, and they had plenty of water in the tender. The Swindon crew complained that they had been waiting in sidings half the night as they had been told by the shed master that there was a report from the RAF station at Lyneham that a German raider was in the vicinity looking for trains; then they thought they saw an aircraft and the signalman shut down the lights and showed a red lamp to warn the enginemen that danger was high in the skies. The crew got down and sheltered under the engine with their tin helmets on for cover, as they were told that they might be strafed and machine-gunned, and a loose bomb was dropped at Swindon before they left.

The Reading relief men discovered that the engine was 'Saint' Class No 2975 *Lord Palmer*, a 4-6-0 two-cylinder engine normally used for passenger trains. The fireman once more took the empty billycans to the station to fill them with cold water and ran back, not spilling a drop. Driver and fireman looked over the footplate; it was in good order with plenty of coal in the tender, most broken down but still some large lumps underneath – they would be sorted out later. The tender hand brake and vacuum brake were found to be working satisfactory after a short test. The fireman placed the billycans on the shelf above the firebox to help warm the water for a cuppa. They waited for the guard's signal of a white lamp and for the signal to drop, indicating that the line was clear and they could move off from the station onto the main line on their way back to Didcot, their last stop.

At 10.40pm they 'got the board' from the signalman together with a white light showing at the rear of the goods train from the guard, so the driver pulled the whistle chain twice and they slowly moved away, with the sand lever pulled to release sand onto the rail to help the driving wheels to grip. They were heading back towards North Junction at Didcot, where they would be relieved by Didcot men, then the train was destined for Bordesley in Birmingham. However, they only got as far as the outskirts of Wantage Road station before being put onto the Up Relief line. The signal was at 'stop' and they were protected by a set of catch points against them; the main line had to be kept clear for the wartime passenger traffic that was passing continuously. They would have to sit there for some time and await a 'path'.

The fireman put the billycans closer to the firebox door while the driver filled in his engine note book with the time of the change-over with the Swindon crew and what time they had left

Challow station with No 2899. The fireman then got down on his knees and crawled through the cab blackout tarpaulin sheet to the top of the tender and started to break up the coal with a pickaxe, making the lumps small enough to get onto the shovel; he also pulled and pushed the coal down closer to the footplate, then with the prep hose connected to the boiler steam pipe he sprayed the tender with water to keep the dust down. He then stoked the fire in the firebox, raking, pushing and pulling with the long metal pricker. This was 10 feet long and an inch thick, and the end that went into the fire was bent into an 'L' shape. He moved the pricker around the firebox to move the clinker and ash, allowing them to drop into the ashpan, then he replaced the pricker in the slot on the tender, glowing white hot. Next he shovelled some fresh Welsh coal into the centre of the firebox, and put on the blower to draw the smoke off and get the footplate warm with a glow that would take the chill off them both. Shutting the blower, he left the firebox doors open just a little to stop the glow on the footplate being seen from the sky, which would be quite dangerous for them with a goods train.

The steam gauge needle started to rise to 225lb per square inch and he kept a eye on the boiler water, as he did not want to

During wartime the glare from the locomotive's firebox had to be masked by a 'Zeppelin sheet'.

fall asleep in the warm environment on the footplate while waiting to move up in the queue of trains; it got quite warm sitting and waiting, and his eyelids started to droop. The men were feeling hungry now, so they got the spare shovel down from the tender, wiped it clean, opened their satchels and pulled out some greaseproof paper containing bacon and a cardboard box with some eggs. They spread the bacon and eggs on the shovel with a lump of lard and placed it in the mouth of the firebox. Meanwhile the billycans were taken from the firebox shelf, the lids removed and tea leaves stirred into the hot water to make a brew. Removing the shovel from the outer ring of the firebox, they both tucked into the hot grub and drank the tea.

The short distance from Challow to Didcot's West Curve was only 11 miles, but it would take them 2¼ hours. They finally got to Foxhall Junction signal box, west of Didcot, and saw a goods trains start to move in front of them. Soon after this West Curve came in sight. As they ran over the tight

curve all the wheel flanges squealed against the rails, despite the Mills Hurcol Lubricator ejecting grease onto the rail edges to stop the noise. The mixed goods train was now running several hours late, but it was not the fault of the enginemen – just wartime conditions.

Above: A Mills Hurcol lubricator. When wheel flanges are tight against the rail on curves, grease is ejected onto the side of the rail to stop the squealing noise. *R. J. Russell collection*

Below: The West Curve at Didcot looking towards Foxhall Junction. The entrance to Didcot Ordinance Depot is on the right. *Adrian Vaughan collection*

The Didcot crew

The following account is from former railwayman and author Harold Gasson.

In December 1941 Driver C. G. 'Charlie' Forbe had transferred from the Southern Region at Weymouth Depot and was posted to Didcot, moving into the railway hostel there. He didn't know that, when he went on shift and left his room, the night shift man would use it, getting into bed after washing himself; there weren't many rooms. Didcot was short of locomen, and they came from all over, from South Wales, Plymouth, London and Fishguard, as excess enginemen within their depots, to help keep the wartime railway working. Didcot shed was relatively newly built, being only about six years old. Driver Forbe was issued with a Second World War tin helmet and a shoulder-strapped box with a gas mask inside; he had to sign for them in the Office Book that was kept with the Register. As with all other locomen, he had to take the equipment out with him on his working shifts in case a rogue German plane should strafe or bomb the engines at Didcot.

He learned the roads very quickly and his main-line duties, and was liked within the shed by the other drivers and firemen – no one had any grief about him, or indeed any of the new arrivals that came to work there, there was such a great demand for all new railwaymen. He was a very quiet man, aged 45, and in good health. He signed the 'Knowledge of the Road book' following several duties running to Reading and Swindon and returning to Didcot, then on to Oxford, learning the loop lines and procedures on dayshift and nightshift runs with freight trains. He made several runs through the new Goods Loop line at Didcot during daytime on 8 August and again on 17 September; on ten occasions in sole charge of his train he proceeded along the Down Goods Loop towards Appleford on shunting duties within the Baltic Yards, Dardanelles Sidings and Centre Yard, as well as the Carriage Sidings.

Didcot shed's allocation of locomotives, January 1942

0-6-0T: Nos 655, 850, 907, 1861, 2021, 2076, 2783, 2787, 2790, 3622, 3677, 4601, 5710, 5735, 5744, 5752, 7709, 7710, 9781

0-6-0: LMS 2F Nos 3108, 3121, 3485, 3564; GWR Nos 2202, 2222, 2251, 2276, 2282, 2289, 2301, 2573

2-6-2T: No 6106

2-4-0: M&SWJR No 1334, one of 11 sold to the Army Ordnance Depot

2-6-0: Nos 4318, 4326, 5397, 6379

4-4-0: 'Bulldog' No 3376 *River Plym*, 3408 *Bombay*, 3448 *Kingfisher*; 'Duke' No 3283 *Comet*; 'Earl' Nos 3206, 3215

4-6-0: Nos 4914 *Cranmore Hall*, 5935 *Norton Hall*, 6923 *Croxteth Hall*

A page from a driver's and fireman's booking on and off book from 1962. *John Pritchard collection*

Driver Forbe had been allocated to 'Zone Relief duties', mostly working freight trains from 'one point to another point', and increased his knowledge and road learning working freight trains to Oxford, running through the Down Goods Loop and noticing the position of catch points and signals – he was a very experienced driver. He always read the notice boards for route changes and special notices when he booked on shift, and helped the firemen working with him. A sight test was due after 12 months at the shed, which found his eyesight normal, including his colour vision; all was tested and passed, and the paperwork signed off and placed in the office in his file.

The shed master at Didcot gave Driver Forbe a high recommendation for his knowledge and as being a reliable and trustworthy driver. His daily record of his turns and time out of the shed and departure of his train were always neatly written in his engine book, right down to the fine detail. He had a clear record; he had left the service in 1913, two years after his first appointment as a engine cleaner, but had then returned six years later while at Weymouth Depot on the Southern Region.

On several occasions Driver Forbe worked with Fireman Jarvis and Freight Guard Mr L. Walker, also a Didcot man. These guards were the salt of the earth; some would even go onto the footplate and fire the engine, and they shared each other's food while working goods trains together. All three men were stationed at Didcot.

Fireman R. A. Jarvis was only 18 years of age and was well liked within Didcot shed. He was described as a smart young fireman, always clean and well dressed with his trousers always tucked into his socks, to stop coal dust getting into his socks and toes, and with very clean working boots. He kept the footplate spick and span, and the Welsh coal was broken down with a pickaxe and sprayed with water to stop the dust blowing into the enginemen's faces, and also to stop small fires starting underneath the coal. Part of his work was getting as much done as possible and helping the driver wherever possible to get the engine off shed within the allowed 45 minutes prep time.

On the night of 12 November 1942 Driver Forbe left the hostel and walked to the station, through the pedestrian tunnel and up the concrete stairs, across the sleeper walkway then down the dusty cinder track to the shed. On arrival the time clerk signed him in, and he then looked at the glass-fronted notice boards to see if there were any restrictions that might change their route to Bordesley.

That night there was initially no sign of Fireman Jarvis. Charlie stepped into the dark night outside the office area and walked up the cinder path to see if he was on his way to work, but there was no sign of him anywhere. So he went in to see the Duty Shed Foreman to see who was available to do the shift with him. The only person who was on shift was the duty shed fireman, Harold Gasson, and he was happy to work with Driver Forbe. He was looking forward to the run as he had worked with Charlie before; he was a nice chap, cheerful and a good driver to fire for. He had told him about all the rough trips he had done on heavy gradients, and how to treat an engine.

Their orders were to relieve a goods train in the Down Relief 'Gully' on the West Curve at Didcot North Junction. When they arrived at the head of the train they found that the engine was 'Saint' Class No 2975 *Lord Palmer*. The two men looked at each other and couldn't believe it. She was straight out of the works after overhaul, and what a treat she looked; she was one of the 'Twenty-Nines' with a straight frame and a Churchward cab. However, it was her condition that really took their breath away; she was just out of Swindon, painted Brunswick Green, and being run in before being released back to the main line. The wooden floorboards were clean as a whistle, with no stains or coal dust in the joints – they could hardly believe their luck.

The Reading engine crew were very upset to see the Didcot men coming up the side steps, because they rarely had a locomotive as perfect as this one. They asked if they could take the train on to the end of the

Above: 'Saint' Class 4-6-0 No 2975 *Lord Palmer* a passenger engine. Built in March 1905 as No 175, the locomotive's first shed allocation was Bristol Bath Road. It was named *Viscount Churchill* in 1907, and renamed *Sir Ernest Palmer* in February 1924, then *Lord Palmer* in October 1933. This engine was involved in the incident with No 4086 *Builth Castle* at Appleford Crossing on 13 November 1942. Its last shed allocation was Banbury and it was withdrawn in November 1944. *Great Western Trust collection*

Right: No member of the 'Saint' Class has been preserved, but this is being rectified by new-build No 2999 *Lady of Legend*. The cab is seen here in course of construction.

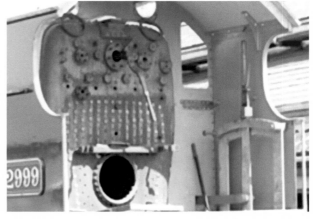

journey; Driver Forbe guessed that they fully expected to go through to Banbury with her, and they were not all that keen to hand it over to the Didcot enginemen. An argument ensued before, very reluctantly, the Reading men left the footplate.

After Charlie and his fireman Harold had had a good look around, they blew the Great Western whistle to alert the signalman that they were ready to move off, then within a few minutes the signal dropped. As they were just about to open the regulator to pull away a shout came from the ground in the dark – it was Driver Forbe's fireman Jarvis, out of breath, having run from the shed across

all the tracks. As he climbed up onto the footplate he explained what had happened – he had slept in. Harold, the relief fireman, therefore collected up his belongings with his helmet and gas mask and climbed down to return to the shed. He was sorry to be leaving the engine, standing there panting as if she was alive, ready to move off. But he had other work to do, perhaps preparing another engine or keeping the stationary boiler going for the heating and hot water. Nonetheless he felt cheated, as it could have been him on that sparkling footplate; what he didn't realise at that moment was that Fireman Jarvis had saved his life.

Countdown to disaster

The Bordesley goods train had come to a stop at North Junction signal box at 12.56am. In the box was signalman Eric Membury, who had received the 'Is Line Clear?' signal from Foxhall Junction at 12.46am, and 'Train Entering Section' at 12.52am, the train arriving at his Home

Jarvis climbed down into the 'six foot', the area between the adjacent tracks, and walked back to the second and third wagons, shouting to the driver to reverse slightly to close up the buffers. Then Guard Walker climbed between the wagons and released the coupling link, letting it drop against the wagon frame. Climbing out onto the path

Eric Membury looks from the window of Didcot North Signal Box – note the painted camouflage 'trees' still visible. In the 1960s his colleagues here were Bill Reynolds and Jack Gardiner. *Marcella Irving collection*

signal 4 minutes later. Signalman Membury reported that, 'I did not know this train had to do work until it arrived, but it generally stops for this purpose or for having relief and I kept the signals at Danger. The goods train came to a stop in the "Relief Gully" and had to shunt into the yard as requested.'

When the train arrived the foreman at West Curve marshalling yard rang North Junction and asked him if it was the 2.30pm Swindon as it had wagons to pick up from the Central Yard. Signalman Membury pulled off the Home signal while the guard walked up to the enginemen to ask for help in releasing the first two wagons. Fireman

A three-link coupling. *Author's collection*

he and the fireman walked back together towards the engine and both climbed the steps onto the footplate. The engine and two wagons went over the points and backed into the yard to do the necessary shunting. The engine had been in the yard for about 10 to

12 minutes when the foreman called to the signalman, Eric Membury, on the 'omnibus' telephone system and told him the train was ready to come out. The engine came out of the Central Yard pulling 12 extra goods and box wagons.

Driver Forbe shunted the new wagons back onto the original rake, pushing up against the buffers to allow Guard Walker to crawl between the wagons and connect them up. Walker then walked back to his guard's van to write out his report. The added wagons made the train up to 73 goods vehicles in total; they were unbraked and loose coupled, and with the guard's van weighing 16 tons the train weight would be about 770 tons, plus the weight of the engine and tender, making 882 tons in all. The length of the train was 511 yards.

As the Down Goods Loop was clear, Signalman Membury 'got the road' for the train from Appleford Crossing at 1.34am, and pulled off all signals for it to proceed. The train pulled slowly past the box, and Eric wondered why it was approaching at such a low speed; then he observed the guard giving a hand signal to the driver, who got the signal just as the engine was outside the box. The train entered the loop at 1.39am, and Eric sent 'Train On Line' to Appleford. Eric reported that, 'My box is just over 100 yards from the loop points and it appeared to me that the train was entering the loop at normal speed. I gave "Train Out of Section" to Foxhall Junction when the van passed my loop starter at 1.43am.'

Meanwhile Signalman

Membury had accepted the 12.00 midnight Paddington to Birkenhead passenger train from Didcot East Junction at 1.38am and received 'Train Entering Section' at 1.43am. He sent the 'Is Line Clear?' signal to Appleford Crossing at 1.38am, then 'Train Entering Section' at 1.44am, at the same time sending 'Train Out of Section' to Didcot East Junction.

Eric said, 'The passenger train passed my box about 1 minute after the van of

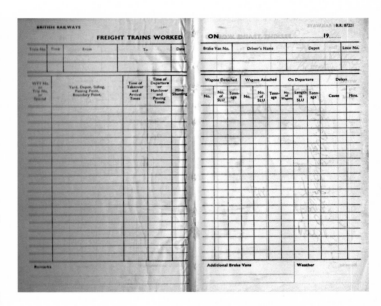

In books such as this a guard kept a record of freight trains worked.

A GWR 20-ton brake van. *R. J. Russell collection*

the goods train had passed. The passenger train was travelling at normal speed, which I should estimate at just over 40 miles per hour.'

Meanwhile the 7.55pm Sheffield to Swindon train was approaching from the north. Eric received the 'Is Line Clear?' signal from Appleford Crossing and accepted it at 1.42am, at the same time that Foxhall Junction accepted the train. 'Train Entering Section' was received at 1.44am, and 'Train Entering Section' sent to Foxhall and 'Train Out of Section' to Appleford at 1.46am, the Birkenhead train having by this time cleared the junction.

The Down Goods Loop at Didcot North Junction was a wartime addition to accommodate slow freight traffic and allow faster passenger trains to pass on the main line. But wartime conditions meant a slow shift for the men working the goods trains, not knowing where they would be relieved or at what time they would get home. Some engine crews got to know the signalmen well

and would meet up for a drink in the local bar or British Railways hostels when off duty.

'Permissive' working was in force over the loop between Didcot North Junction signal box and Appleford Crossing. In accordance with the Great Western Railway's Permissive Block Regulations, goods running loops were subject to a general speed restriction of 10mph, and it was laid down that in all cases, irrespective of the state of the weather, enginemen must regard the lowering of the signal to enter the loop only as an indication that the points were set in the proper position, and must not expect that the road would be clear through the loop; they would be held responsible for stopping their train short of any obstruction that might be in front of them.

Didcot North Junction box controlled the facing points and signals at the entrance to the loop, while the trailing connection and signals at the exit were worked by Appleford Crossing. The layout was such that a train from the Swindon direction

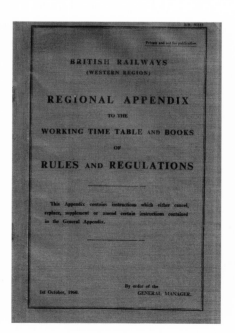

The working timetable and the Rules and Regulations governing all aspects of railway operation were continually updated.

This is Didcot North Junction signal box looking towards Oxford. The wooden shed on the right was used by locomen waiting for goods trains; it had a small potbelly stove inside to keep it warm and to heat food and drinks. A frying pan sat on the table with mouse and rat droppings in it – enginemen thought they were currants! *Harold Gasson collection*

could be admitted to the loop and proceed as far as the catch points signal at the same time as a train from the London direction was signalled through on the Down Main, as occurred in this case. The facing trap points, at which the freight train was derailed, consisted of a pair of switches and turnout rails; the lead rail in the 'four foot' (the space between the rails) terminated in a wood block covered with a steel plate, level with the inside of the access rail. Owing to the level crossing 70 yards ahead of the catch points, there was no room for an effective 'sand drag' to catch an overrunning train.

In the construction of the Down Goods Loop special care had been taken to provide

Above: In this closer view of North Junction, the signal on the left indicates the start of the Down Goods Loop. The tracks on the right were those used by the northbound Birkenhead train coming from Didcot East Junction. *Adrian Vaughan collection*

Right: Looking in the opposite direction towards North Junction, the nearest signal controls access to the Down Goods Loop from the Down Main. The Down Goods Loop is on the extreme right, and the Up Goods Loop on the extreme left. *Adrian Vaughan collection*

sufficient clearance for the Down Main and Down Loop signals to be sited to the left of their respective lines. The curvature, however, for a train proceeding along the loop from the Swindon direction was continuously left-handed, which adversely affected the view of the signals from the driver's position on the right-hand side of the footplate, as was standard on the GWR.

With reference to the accompanying diagram, the engine of the freight train started from point 'B', after attaching some wagons from the yard. The next signal applying to this train was the bracket signal 'C', which controlled the entrance

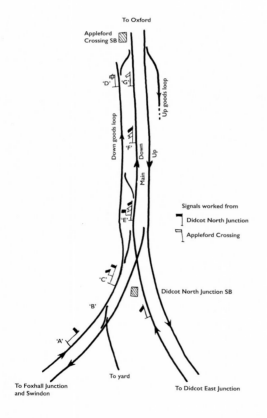

to the loop, and whose left-hand arm was lowered. It was claimed in the report into the accident that from the starting point, signal 'C' was barely visible through the right-hand side cab window, clear of the front corner of the engine firebox, and from the fireman's side it was masked by the twin posts of the same nearby up line signals. Onwards from the starting point, signal 'C' was screened from the driver's view by the boiler, but was clearly visible from the fireman's side until it was passed.

There were no further signals applicable to the loop until the train reached signal 'D', which was at Danger, and the catch points. However, the bracket signal 'E', which controlled the entrance to the loop from the Down Main, would come into the driver's view when proceeding into the loop from the Swindon direction at about the same time as he lost sight of the signal 'C', or a little after; he would see signal 'F' then signal 'G', each at a range of 500 yards. Owing to the left-hand curvature, the loop outlet signal 'D' was not visible from the driver's side of the footplate until the engine was approximately 220 yards from it, but it could be seen for approximately 1,000 yards from the fireman's side, although it was obscured from time to time by a heavy telegraph pole route on the left. The left-hand arm of signal 'C' for entering the loop had a 4-inch lens in its lamp compared to the standard 6-inch lens for main-line signals. The outlet signal 'D' had a 4-inch lens, and its signal arm carried a ring, indicating that it referred to a subsidiary line.

When Driver Forbe entered the Down Goods Loop he had either not remembered or had not realised that it was on a falling gradient, and Guard Walker sensed that the train was going slightly faster than normal, so wound down his hand brake, screwing it down harder than normal, trying to slow the train. He had worked this route several times, and had gone through the loop on other occasions. The speed restriction was 10mph, and the train appeared to be travelling at 25mph. He thought that Driver

A simplified sketch plan of the track layout at Didcot North Junction, showing the lines used by the two trains involved in the accident and the signals controlling their passage (not to scale). The Down Goods Loop towards Appleford Crossing was just over 1,200 yards long and was brought into use in October 1941, 13 months before the accident.

to the other, and both engines blew their whistles, that characteristic Great Western sound that echoed across the countryside.

Signalman Eric Membury's statement related that, 'At 5.08am I received a box-to-box message that the breakdown vans had left Reading at 4.55am. The vans arrived via the Down Northern Loop at 5.58am and went into the section on the up road at 6.45am. The Didcot breakdown vans were withdrawn from the section at 6.25am to allow the Old Oak Common vans to be placed in position. The engine was allowed to enter the section on the Down Road at 6.35am with a "Wrong Line Order" for the purpose of withdrawing the rear coach of the 12.00 midnight Paddington, which was placed in the yard at 7.03am. I left duty at 7.00am having stayed on an extra hour to acquaint my relief with the exact position.'

Signalman Gough at Appleford Crossing had been on duty for 3½ hours, during which time no other train had run through the Down Goods Loop. After accepting the goods train he maintained the Stop signal at 'Danger', intending to hold the train in the loop until the Birkenhead express had passed. He accepted the latter at 1.38am and noted in his Train Register Book that he received 'Line Clear' from the box ahead at 1.39am and immediately lowered all the down line signals, including the two Distants. With regard to the few moments before the derailment and collision, Signalman Gough stated at the inquiry:

'I could see the headlights of the train approaching my box, which to my mind should have been the goods train, but because of the rate of speed at which it was approaching I thought it must be the passenger train. The headlights of the engine appeared to be close together for "A" headlights. I opened the sash window as I thought the glass might be deceiving me. I could then see it was the goods train and almost at the same time I saw the lights of the passenger train approaching on the down main line. I realised that the goods train would run through the catch points. When the crash took place I immediately placed my signals to "Danger" and sent the "Obstruction Danger" signal in both directions at 1.46am.'

Signalman Gough also said that he made a practice of verifying that the light of the Stop signal was burning properly before accepting a train into the loop; on this occasion he did so by observing the signal's backlight. He did not notice whether the freight train was running under steam. However, the regulator of the overturned engine was found to be closed, with the vacuum brake fully applied with the reversing screw in forward gear at the 45% cut-off position.

Signalman Gough, having witnessed the derailment and crash, made the first call for assistance. Rescue operations were soon in place, and Great Western Railway staff began to arrive from Didcot within several minutes.

Appleford Crossing.

Signalman Jack Gough at Appleford in 1942.

On board the passenger train were Army and RAF personnel going to their bases or home on leave, and they started to clear away the wreckage trying to get to the trapped people in their seats, working as a team to free those who were badly trapped. There was very little delay in removing the injured to hospital.

Although the site was isolated, ambulances and medical staff from Didcot, Abingdon, Oxford and Wallingford arrived between the hours of 2.30am and 3.30am. It was a cold night, and mobile canteens of the YMCA and the WVS rendered valuable service in providing hot drinks for the unhurt passengers who stood around waiting for transport to continue their journeys.

The 11 bogie vehicles of the express passenger train were all of modern construction with heavy steel underframes and wooden-framed bodies. Their total weight was 330½ tons. The engine was GWR four-cylinder 'Castle' 4-6-0 No 4086 Builth Castle, built at Swindon in 1925 and scrapped in 1962; she weighed 126½ tons in working order with tender, so the combined weight of the Birkenhead train was 457 tons with a total length of 250 yards. Five coaches of the passenger train had came into violent sidelong collision with the wreckage of three vans and 17 wagons of the goods train that had been derailed and fallen towards the Down Main; 13 of them were smashed beyond repair and a further 10 suffered varying degrees of damage.

The bogies of the third and fourth coaches were severely damaged, and those of the fifth was demolished. A gap of about 150 yards separated the front portion of the train from the six remaining passenger coaches; the front portion came to rest opposite Appleford Crossing signal box about 60 yards ahead of the trailing connection of the Down Goods Loop. The first five vehicles were derailed, but they remained coupled and partially in line, and there was no telescoping, although one was partially overturned to the right. There was extensive

damage to their bodywork, mainly on the left-hand side, as well as to the bogies and undergear, but the sixth stopped almost clear, and was neither derailed nor seriously damaged.

The permanent way, sleepers and ballast were considerably damaged, with the rails twisted and buckled from the force of the engine, tender and goods wagons that wrenched them out of their securing chairs as if they were a soft metal, skewing the wooden sleepers sideways and out of shape zigzagging down towards the crossing gates.

The lines were cleared by 2.50pm the following day, 14 November, and normal working was resumed on the two main lines after 39 hours, but both loops were occupied for some time with the wreckage of the crashes.

The following Sunday morning, 15 November, Lord Palmer was dragged out of the field, rerailed and brought back to Didcot shed, being towed by a 'Hall' and shunted next to the shed on No 5 road. She was not badly damaged, but her left side was covered in mud, and her cab bent with the hand-rails twisted. Harold Gasson with other Didcot men climbed up on the footplate and found that her boiler was covered in coal dust where the tender had crashed on top of the engine, and dry mud was splattered over the clean footplate boards. She was as cold as ice. The enginemen left her, some expressing the sorrow that was in their hearts, and she was taken away and never seen again. The death of the two fine men was keenly felt, not only at Didcot but also at all other Great Western Railway sheds, even those of other companies, because enginemen were one big railway family. Enginemen knew that when all the glamour of handling a steam engine was swept aside, being on a large locomotive with maybe more than a thousand tons moving behind could be a tough occupation. They were all brothers, whether on the footplate or on the fitting side at the shed. They were all bonded together by steam engines.

Chapter 2
Moreton marshalling yard

In 1940-42 the vicinity of Didcot, with all the junctions, signal boxes and railway lines, were assigned for upgrades because of the Second World War and the anticipated wartime traffic. Extra loop lines were laid in beside the Down Main and Up Main in the Appleford area. Didcot North Junction, Foxhall Junction and East Junction boxes were all extended and given extra levers. When North Junction signal box was extended it was painted with green and brown trees, covering the new brickwork as camouflage; German bombers and fighters might approach low over the tracks and drop a lucky bomb somewhere in the nearby Ordinance Depot. The camouflage stayed on the box for many years, well into the 1960s.

Train movement regulators were employed at Didcot East Junction signal box from 1942 to regulate the movement of the important war supply trains and to avoid long delays through the large complex of junctions, reporting all movements from the north, south, east and west to Reading Control. To help with the working of the very busy East Junction signal box, it was a two-signalman job; one handled all the up traffic and most of shunting movements at the east end of the station, while the other handled all the down traffic. There was also a booking boy at East Junction, who dealt with the logging of each train movement, recording them in the

Train Register Book, as well as answering a battery of 19 different telephones. The box was a Special C class.

The Great Western Railway's marshalling yard in the rural location of North Moreton Cutting near Didcot was begun in 1940 to act as an overflow and take the pressure off the yard at Reading, and to help with the huge increase in freight that was anticipated as a result of the war.

The new yard was located opposite Fulscot Farm a mile or so east of Didcot. No heavy machinery was available to dig out the trenches and lay the drainage pipes, or tracked bulldozers to move the earth, just wheelbarrows, picks, shovels and spades, and, of course, manpower. Heavy concrete pipes had to be installed between the gully of the embankment and the new yard; after digging out by hand the construction men rigged a rope pulley block system and lowered the pipes into the ground, covered the ends with a concrete paste and finished with a skimmed concrete liner. The drainage water flowed directly into a dug-out hole on the other side of the bridge.

The extended Didcot North Junction signal box, with Signalman Eric Membury at the window.

Moreton Yard under construction. *Science and Society Picture Library*

The spoil removed was used to make extra embankments for the tracks into the goods loops around the Didcot complex. Extra goods lines were constructed from Fulscot Bridge, North Moreton, to Marsh Bridge towards Didcot East Junction signal box, then the East Goods Loop, ending at Appleford Crossing. Another Goods Loop was also constructed near Foxhall Junction signal box taking goods trains away from the main lines and allowing passenger trains to run unimpeded on the Up and Down main lines. The

Alec Membury was signalman at Moreton Cutting signal box, extended when the new yard was built.

last embankment was at the entrance to the Didcot, Newbury & Southampton (DN&S) line, where extra tracks were laid to Churn estate, again taking heavy goods trains away from the main line and out into the country; the line also provided a useful short cut to Southampton.

Soon many goods trains were arriving at the new marshalling yard owned by Reading, where 16 roads had been laid; they came from all directions, the North, the Midlands, west from Reading, and south from Newbury. On arrival up to 120 wagons could be sorted off each train with a guard's van at each end. The working shifts for the shunting crews were 24 hours a day, seven days a week. In 1943 the signal box at Moreton Cutting was upgraded to 90 levers with the extra connections to the marshalling yard, and three shifts allowed work to continue for 24 hours seven days a week.

In early 1942 the water system was connected to supply the water columns.

Swindon-built tank engines were newly allocated to Didcot shed, Nos 3622, 5700 and 5735; these were strong locomotives capable of shunting rakes of 20-ton wagons, sometimes shunting 60 at a time up the back of the yard towards one of the four concrete stop blocks where the 'tanky' would push them together and compress the buffers with sufficient force that the shunters could couple and uncouple them, the powerful engines slipping and sliding as they did so.

So successful was the initial yard that the railway bought the rest of the adjacent field and extended it. This time little earthworks were required; the sleepers and tracks were laid on the ground and a hump was built to allow wagons to run down and be sorted into the various roads. Another 'tanky' was required, and they all worked hard 24 hours a day. The yard opened in 1943 to accommodate the increasing numbers of freight trains and help with the invasion of Europe.

Shunters at Moreton yard: second from the left standing on the board is Bill Membury. *Reg Warr collection*

Of the 16 roads, Nos 1 and 2 were the reception roads. The others were numbered and named as follows: No 3 Hayes; No 4 Maidenhead and Slough; No 5 Basingstoke; No 6 exchange road; No 7 Sonning Power Station; No 8 Southern at Reading; No 9 Tonbridge; No 10 Feltham; No 11 Redhill; No 12 Taplow; No 13 Reading West

Junction; No 14 Reading High Level; No 15 Reading Low Level; and No 16 cripple sidings. Two 'tankies' sorted all the traffic that came into the yard, one working roads 1 to 5, the front yard, and the other working roads 7 to 16, the back yard. A coal truck was sent to supply the 'tankies' when they ran low.

Left: Workers at the yard needed to carry an Identification Card in case they were stopped and accused of spying! *The late Cyril Tolley collection*

Below: Didcot-allocated pannier tanks Nos 5752 and 907.

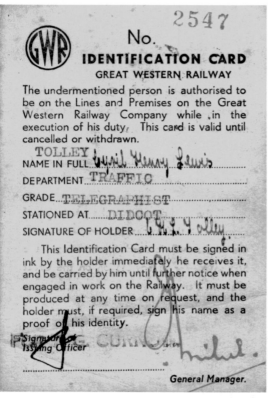

Moreton yard filled to the brim with general goods and coal for the furnaces during the Second World War in 1943. *Both R. J. Russell collection*

Jimmy Holmar

Lewis Holmar has memories of his father working in the Running & Maintenance section at Didcot Shed, which was coded 81E. In the 1940s Jimmy used to commute from Hanney Road in Steventon village near Abingdon. Then the family moved and lived in wooden barracks huts at the old Army Camp at the top end of Didcot for eight years until they were allocated one of the new semi-detached houses that were built for the council in Harding Strings. This was a new development for the overflow of people coming to Didcot at that time in the 1940s and '50s as a result of the shortage of men on the railways.

'We moved into a brand-new house in 1953 in Harding Strings, Didcot,' remembers Lewis. 'I slept in the front bedroom and would be woken up by the guy known as the

"knocker-upper", sent out to get the fitters and others down to the shed if there was a breakdown or derailment any time at night, sometimes at 2 or 3 in the morning. This was in the days of thick smog and freezing fog. Dad would get dressed, jump on his bike and away he went without any breakfast. It meant that Mum would get up and make some "doorstep" cheese sandwiches or occasionally boiled bacon. Later I would go out in the back garden to the shed and pick up a large potato and a couple of onions, put them in a bag, then cycle down to the station, walk through the subway and across the carriage marshalling yard to the loco shed, letting the tally or token man know that I was down with food for my Dad and his mate, who happened to be Matt Oglesby.

'The cabin had a coke stove. I would empty the ashpan and place the potatoes and onions in the bottom of the stove to cook, keeping an eye on the stove till the breakdown van came back to the shed.

'A few of us railwaymen's sons were privileged in having the freedom to be in and around the railway. I even used to help a Polish man fill the tenders with coal, shovelling coal from the coal wagons in the coal stage into small iron boxes on wheels. Each held a ton of coal, which was then tipped over the ledge sticking out over the tender; the flap would open and the coal flow out into the tender. The coal dust blew about everywhere.

'I remember being shocked to hear sometime later that Dad and a few others had been to the lake by the Provender Stores with drag lines to retrieve the body of that really kind man – they found his clothes neatly folded at the side of the lake.

'The men carried such burdens with

Jimmy Holmar.

them after the horrors of war – I guess the camaraderie of the railway and was a great safety valve for them. All I can add as a railwayman's son is that it gave us an amazing insight into the future of our working lives and the knowledge and responsibility needed in the workplace.

'Together with many others, Dad was in attendance of the awful derailment at Milton, west of Didcot, on Sunday 20 November 1955, which cost so many lives and injuries. He was in the wreckage first followed by a doctor; he made space as best he could so that the doctor was able to comfort each casualty that they found. The emergency services found the best way to unlock the entangled wreckage so as not to cause more suffering to those entombed within. Dad was there for several days until the needs of all had been attended to.

'I have a letter of thanks from the railway bosses for Dad's services during that event. I know it affected all of them that worked in

BRITISH TRANSPORT COMMISSION

H. E. A. WHITE, A.M.I. MECH. E.
Motive Power Superintendent
H. G. KERRY, M.I. Mech.E.
Assistant Motive Power Superintendent
Telephone M.
SWINDON 2611
Ext 2383
Telegraphic Address
POWER RAILWAY SWINDON

MOTIVE POWER SUPERINTENDENT WESTERN REGION SWINDON, WILTS

B.R. 32600/28

Our Reference M.2242   Thursday, 15th December, 1955
Your Reference 1.
PERSONAL.

Dear Mr Holmar,

         Our General Manager, Mr Grand, was extremely well pleased with the work of this Department on the occasion of the unfortunate accident at Milton on Sunday, November 20th. He has asked me to pass his personal appreciation to all staff involved.

         I would like to add my own appreciation and thanks for your part in the operation.

              Yours faithfully.

Fitter I. Holmar,
Didcot

The letter of thanks from the railway bosses following Jimmy's work helping in the aftermath of the Milton crash.

close proximity – it had the same effect on them as the war. I was lucky to have amazing parents.'

Lewis recalls that he had some precious times with the author's father, especially in the boxing gym (of which more later) – 'he really sharpened me up'.

John Pritchard

'It was a late summer evening in 1961,' remembers loco fireman John, 'as I was working a loose-coupled train to Didcot over the Didcot, Newbury & Southampton line. The engine was "Mogul" No 6379. We saw that the road was against us as we approached the junction with the main line at Didcot East Junction. My mate Dick Hooper started to brake and the loose-coupled train closed up, then surged forward because of the falling gradient. Dick blew the whistle to alert the guard but to no avail – we just kept going. Most guards were very good at assisting in stopping a train by applying the van brake. But a few just got their heads down to sleep as soon as the train was moving.

'We were about half a mile from the junction and still travelling too fast. Dick was starting to panic, saying, "You may have to pin down some of the brakes."

'Passing a signal at Danger was one of the most serious offences a driver could commit, so I grabbed the coal pick and managed to jump onto the ground without falling over. I guess we were travelling at 8-10mph but it seemed a lot faster. I managed to pin down about eight wagon brakes using the pick handle as a lever, but the train kept on moving. Dick was now hanging on both whistle chains – we were definitely not going to stop. Then at the last moment the signalman gave us the road. I unpinned the eight wagons, and scrambled back aboard.

'A relief crew took over the train at North Junction. The new driver blew the whistle and was given the road towards Oxford straight away. As the guard's van passed us Dick shouted something unprintable towards the van, but there was still no sign of the guard – he was probably still asleep, completely unaware that for a while he was in charge of a runaway train.'

On another occasion John remembers a gang of platelayers shouting to him as he was passing them to 'Drop us off some coal, mate!' This happened from time to time because they needed it for use in their lineside cabins.

'I was working a goods train from Newbury to Reading and the request took place near Aldermaston. We were travelling at about 30mph. I checked the tender and found a rather large oval-shaped lump of coal – it must have weighed about 100lb. As we drew near to the lineside hut I noticed that the door was wide open so I decided to throw the coal as close to the hut as possible, thinking it would smash into small pieces as it hit the ground. One good heave and the lump of coal flew off the footplate, hit the footpath and bounced forward like a dam-busting bouncing bomb straight into the open doorway. As we passed there was an enormous bang as the coal smashed through the back of the hut, splinters of wood and coal showering everywhere – the hole was about 3 foot across.

'My mate at the time was Billy Brown, and he witnessed what had happened. Billy suffered with a stutter and said, "F-f-f-flipping hell – don't mention this to anyone." Luckily we never did receive a "Please Explain" memo.'

Author's memories

One day the Fitter Foreman Arthur Brinkley asked me into his office to talk about helping him and training me at the same time to write out daily and weekly reports, while he kept an eye on me. He didn't want to take a fitter or fitter's mate out of the system as we were short of manpower.

My job was to keep records of locomotives and next-day repairs, as well as pulling out the cards and checking the records for each locomotive; this I did and kept my own records for the future. I had

to walk around the front of the shed mid-morning and the dead roads at the side. In the afternoons I had to write the reports and make phone calls to other sheds; I would then go out again and take engine numbers, noting the oval shedplates of foreign sheds, which were fixed underneath the smokebox door. All the sheds had their own plates: Old Oak Common was 81A, Slough was 81B, Southall 81C, Reading 81D and Oxford 81F. Didcot itself was 81E.

When the 'omnibus' phone rang – the exchange was in Didcot station – I had to take the messages and reports from other depots, including foreign sheds as far away as Doncaster or Westbury. I had to take the person's name and telephone number and send back reports. It worked the other way as well, as I had to ring them with details of their engines that had broken down and had to be repaired. Everything I did had to be Arthur's decision – I would wait for his opinion and orders. I enjoyed working in the office, because I was clean.

Another job that arose was taking the measurements of locomotive driving wheel tyre thicknesses; on a 'Hall' Class, for example, that meant the first leading wheel, the driving wheel and the trailing wheel, on both sides of the engine. I made a drawing on a piece of scrap paper marked 'Leading axle', 'Driving axle' and 'Trailing axle', with a cross to indicate the front of the engine. When I got back into the office and cleaned up and washed my hands, I would pull out the locomotive's brown card to write the measurements out.

I kept my own records of these locomotives and their driving wheels and noted them in a notebook small enough to fit into my pocket. After changing into my overalls I went to the stores for a bucket of paraffin and some cotton waste, handing over a chitty for the quantity received. I had a small scraper which I used to scrape the dirt and oil off the rim of the driving wheels. I got a 'Not To Be Moved' red board and placed it on the engine; with luck there was a pit so I could get underneath the engine and scrape off the oil and dirt, making a nice clean rim on the wheel. I then put on the gauge and took the readings from it for each wheel, noting the figures down on my scrap of paper.

This was OK until I had to kneel down to take the measurements, or lay down on the dirty floor or outside in the dead engine area. All people could see was a pair of legs sticking out from the wheel area – it looked like someone had committed suicide!

When the piston and valve rings had to be changed I kept all those records too.

'Brink' was pleased. I was learning and I kept his office, and the records, up to date.

I went over to a carriage and wagon siding for some scrap metal to make tools. Dave Davis taught me, and we made some inside and outside callipers from some old plate, involving plenty of filing and as they took shape.

One job undertaken by fireman was inspection of superheaters. When John came onto the ashpit from the main line the first thing he did was to find an old long-handled broom, tie some cotton waste around the handle, open the smokebox door wide, then shout to the driver that he was ready. The driver would then open the regulator to one notch, having made sure that he had wound the tender hand brake fully down and applied the vacuum brake fully to stop the

A locomotive smokebox, showing the superheater elements in the boiler tubes. *Peter Sedge collection*

engine moving. Feeling the pull of the steam pumping into the cylinders and the engine wanting to move off, John lit the cotton waste with his lighter and, holding the broom at the brush end, poked it into each superheater element to check that the flame was drawn into the tube. He then did the same thing with each superheater element, checking to see if any were faulty. Eventually he pulled the cotton waste off the broom handle and threw the broom down onto the path where he would pick it up later. Shouting to the driver to shut the regulator, John climbed into the smokebox and marked any superheater element that needed to be changed with a cross using a piece of chalk. The driver put this on his inspection card and passed the card to the Shed Foreman, who in turn passed it to the Fitter Foreman, with the fitters, and an apprentice would replace the superheater

Johnny Cooper

The late Johnny Cooper worked in the shed at Didcot as a boilersmith's mate. He originally came from Bristol, and had a girlfriend there, so they broke up. He was a real character – no one took him seriously – and he would always say hello to me every day whenever he was on the day shift.

His eating habits were a bit weird, usually pigs' trotters, cabbage and peeled spuds cut up into quarters, then covered in water and stewed with a couple of Oxo cubes stirred together in a galvanised bucket placed on the pot-belly stove within the rest area. He kept the bucket, covered with a galvanised lid, in his locker in the cabin when he went off shift.

While he worked hard like most of the men inside the shed, outside among the cold or dead engines on Nos 5/6/7/8 roads it was hard to find a boilersmith working until you heard the noise of hammering within an engine firebox and the echoes and curses coming from it. Climbing up onto the footplate and waiting for the shouting to stop, I looked over the other side of the footplate and there below me was the wooden wheelbarrow the smiths used. Seeing what was inside I realised that the work consisted of fitting new firebars. Then the shouting eased slightly and someone popped his head out of the firebox entrance (like a guillotine with his head in it ready to be chopped off!).

It was Johnny Cooper, with a face mask held on by rubber straps holding the air valves over his mouth, and rivers of sweat running down his face. He climbed out onto the footplate wet through, and cursed how hard those firebars had moulded themselves into the slots as a result of the clinker and burning coals; the enormous heat would cause the bars to twist, and the gratings allowed the ash to drop though and collect in the ashpan underneath the firebox.

He asked me whether I had seen Bill Cox on my travels – he was going to help Johnny but it seemed that he had disappeared, as usual.

'I've got to get back inside, Pat – sorry, got to get these bars out as they want this engine tomorrow.'

I did a quick inspection as to what was needed and reported back to Jack Dearlove, the duty fitter, with a list – the engine was No 4959 *Purley Hall*.

Passing the boilersmith's cabin one morning I looked in to see Johnny eating winkles from a brown paper bag using a pin to scrape them out straight into his mouth. My stomach churned – they looked horrible.

He said, 'Help yourself.'

'No thanks…'

One day Johnny came up with a plan when he heard me shouting for Bengy Carter, or Bengy was looking for me in the shed. People started to notice and said, 'What are those two up to again?' His plan was a code of two whistles from the mouth, the answer being the same but three whistles

in a different pitch. It would save shouting around the workshop above the noise. We tried it out between the three of us and, yes, it worked; we used the system all the while until Didcot shed closed, steam was phased out and we went our different ways.

Archie Davies

Everyone remembers Archie! Top link Didcot Driver Lynn Thomas Davies, always known as 'Archie', was born in Neath in South Wales, one of six boys, and married Linda Fisher on 5 October 1946. He started as a cleaner at Neath in 1943, working his way up to become a temporary fireman, getting to know what was what and learning all the time during those wartime years.

Like other firemen from the Welsh Valleys, he found that work was not abundant, but elsewhere there was a shortage of skilled manpower and knowledge, and extra firemen were needed at Didcot and Oxford with all the freight trains moving war materials across the country.

Archie therefore transferred to Oxford as a locomotive fireman, then transferred again within the same year and came to Didcot as a fireman. He got a place in the hostel and met other men that had come up from the same area in South Wales. He became well-liked, and out on the road he was getting to know how the system worked, and earned respect from drivers as a good fireman – except maybe one.

One day young fireman Archie clocked on with Didcot Driver Alf Summers. They had to get their engine ready and 45 minutes prep time was allowed on shed. Checking the water in the tank, Alf said that they did not want any, so Archie took his word and got on with all the jobs required to get the engine ready: collecting tools from dead engines, checking the tool boxes for the tube of detonators and red and green flags, washing down the footplate, and placing the billycans above the firebox to keep warm. Eventually they got the all clear from the Shed Foreman, blew the whistle and pulled out of the shed.

CALL   ANSWER

Archie Davies is on the back row, third from right, with cigarette.

They went up to North Junction signal box to pick up their mixed goods train, backing into the yard and connecting up. When they got the flag from the guard they pulled out, destination north towards Birmingham, where they would change crews. Archie noticed that the water was getting low in the tender and told Alf, but he shook his head and said that they were not stopping. This worried Archie, as the boiler might blow up without water. After a while they were pulled in by a signalman while an express passenger train passed, and with luck there was a water column nearby; they pulled up close and Archie put the canvas bag over the tender's water hole, climbed down onto the ground and opened the valve. Meanwhile Alf stood on the footplate; it seems it was below him to help out.

When they got to their destination they had to walk to the shed and report to the Shed Foreman. They were given an ex-LMS loco, Ivatt 4MT 2-6-0 No 43108, and collected another goods train for the run

back to Oxford, where another crew would take over, then home on a stopper to Didcot. However, there must have been something wrong with the Ivatt as they were having trouble with the water valve from tender to engine – it was sticking – but Archie managed to free it by using the controls. Home was getting nearer, and they signed off late at night.

Next shift Archie drew the short straw once more, and got Alf Summers. While getting their engine ready within the 45-minute prep time, Archie hatched a plan. Meanwhile he got the canvas bag over but was again told that they didn't need water. When the 45 minutes was up, they drew out onto the road to North Moreton marshalling yard, which was operated by Reading; they had to take a goods train to Reading main marshalling yard. Again the water started to get low in the tender and Archie said to

Alf that they needed water, but again he said that they did not. The next thing that happened was that the footplate was full of steam; Archie had undone a sight gauge gland nut plug, and steam poured out of the cab windows. Alf was screaming. Archie said, 'That's what will happen if you don't let me fill the tender with water.' He had to make a report when they got back to the shed; all he stated was that perhaps the injectors had been faulty with the lack of attention during wartime.

There was friction between them from then on, and Alf stopped at every single water column, whether they needed water or not, just to rub it in. Alf died on 2 May 1997.

One day in the 1960s Archie, by now a driver, was at the front of Didcot shed getting his engine ready to proceed out onto the main line to complete his dayshift. The engine was 2-6-0 'Mogul' No 5326, being prepared to the usual high standard, and even though the prep time was being reduced there was still lots to do. Mike Bosley, the fireman, was looking at the steam gauge, with its needle waving in the glass and the pressure rising slowly at 102lb per square inch. The scraper was dragged out of the rack on the tender to scrape back the

clinker before Mike shovelled another load of coal into the firebox. He also washed down the coal to stop combustion at the bottom of the fresh coal in the tender, then with the same hose he started to spray the footplate, having looked out both sides to check that no one was walking by.

Mike's driver for the day was Archie, and he was a happy worker and got on with what was expected of him – he just got his head down and got on with his duties to get her ready. The water column was next on his list. Walking over the coal then down to the frame of the rear of the tender, he opened the water tank lid and dropped it down with a bang. Next he climbed down the iron steps on the rear of the tender onto the buffer beam and dropped to the ground. He then swung the canvas bag to the rear of the tender frame, wrapping the chain tightly round his hand, and climbed back up onto the tender, with all his might pulling the canvas bag into the hole in the tender. Firemen must have been very fit then, up and down all day long.

He got off the engine again as Archie could not be seen to help out, went to the water valve and wound it anti-clockwise to allow the water to gush into the tank. He stood resting for a while until water cascaded

A GWR 2-6-0 'Mogul' of the same class as that driven by Archie when Mike Bosley was firing for him. *Author's collection*

over the sides of the tender, then wound the valve clockwise and shut the handle tight. The water was dripping from the canvas bag as he pulled it back to the resting place on No 4 road.

As he walked past the footplate he noticed that Archie had done the oiling on the con-rods; there was a dribble of fresh oil running down the metal rod. All done, but where was he? The smokebox door was wide open, and on both sides of the engine there were fitters working on the pistons repacking the glands, as steam was escaping from the shaft.

Mike looked up into the smokebox and there was Archie, hammering away inside. Mike asked him what he was doing.

Archie replied, 'F–ed if I know, but all the other drivers do this!'

What a man!

(In fact, he was placing copper wire around the blastpipe and over the top centre to get a better performance out of the engine under steam.)

The full billycans were placed on top of the shelf, and red and green flags with detonators were ready in the tube in the tool box on the tender. They got the 'all clear' from the fitters, and the Shed Foreman, Harry Buckle, with his bowler hat, came out of the office door, walked smartly up to the 'Mogul' and pulled a watch from his waistcoat pocket. At that moment he heard the Great Western whistle sound and the engine pulled away from the front of the shed. Archie waved at him and put his thumb in the air. Time – dead on 45 minutes!

Archie was not happy unless he was driving at speed, and he built up a reputation of which he was proud. His experiences as a train driver ranged from standing at the controls of *Flying Scotsman* to those of 'Thomas the Tank Engine'! Later, in the 1980s and 1990s, he drove many Great Western Society excursions. He retired in 1991 after 48 years of service with the Great Western Railway and British Railways, and sadly has since gone to that railway in the sky!

Not all of Archie's firemen appreciated his love of speed. One, George Fuller from Yeovil, told a story that he put his shovel back in the tender and told Archie he was not working if he drove like that! On another occasion Archie was going up

Archie loved speed. When he was at Oxford he used to work the 5.30pm up train to Paddington non-stop in exactly 60 minutes. His favourite loco for this turn was No 6959 *Peatling Hall*. He would sand the rails while backing on to his train so he got a faster start! I am sure this letter that appeared in the railway press refers to him! Didcot shed foreman Reg Warr told me that such driving was dangerous as there weren't adequate brakes for an emergency stop.

Fastest steam train

Sɪʀ,—I have been a keen student of time-tables for many years. It recently occurred to me that it would be interesting to establish which is now our fastest *steam* train, so I undertook some intensive research on the subject. To my surprise, the honour falls to the Western Region, the train concerned being its 5.30 p.m. from Oxford to Paddington, which covers the 63.5 miles in exactly 60 min. non-stop, at 63.5 m.p.h. I have travelled by this train on several occasions recently, and have witnessed some extremely lively running. On one occasion, a " Hall " class locomotive (deputising for the usual " Castle "), with a load of seven coaches, sustained speeds of 80-83 m.p.h. throughout the 23 miles between mileposts 28 and 5.

H. Swain

Harrow, Middx.

Archie Davies still really enjoyed his driving in the preservation era.

Archie leaves Banbury driving No 6024 *King Edward I* – a typical start!

YOU ARE INVITED TO CELEBRATE
THE RETIREMENT OF
LYNN THOMAS DAVIES

ARCHIE'S
65TH
BIRTHDAY

TO BE HELD AT THE
ABINGDON LODGE HOTEL
IN THE
THAMES ROOM
ON
12TH OCTOBER AT 7.30 PM

THE FLYING WELSHMAN

MENU

VEGETABLE SOUP
PRAWN COCKTAIL

ROAST TURKEY
with vegetables in season

VEGETABLE LASAGNE
with vegetables in season

FRESH FRUIT SALAD
and cream

CHOCOLATE PROFITEROLES
and cream

COFFEE

TOAST

Above left: Didcot Railway Centre was once the home shed of top link driver Archie, seen here on the footplate of preserved No 6024 *King Edward I.*

Left, below left, above and below: Archie celebrated his 65th birthday on 12 October 1991 at Abingdon. I bought a firing shovel at a car boot sale and stuck plastic egg and bacon on it. We also bought him a children's Fisher Price doctor's set, including stethoscope and auroscope, reflecting his interest in medicine.

Savernake Bank tender-first light engine with a 'Hall'. He was about to put her into 45% cut-off at 65mph when the fireman walked over and said to him, 'Please slow down, mate – I'm too young to die !' When Archie was on preserved No 5051 *Earl Bathurst* heading for Banbury and Didcot, he had her at 35% cut-off all the way. As soon as his fireman Tony Neal put 12 shovelfuls of coal into the firebox, Archie wound her up to 40% and it all went up the chimney. Tony Neal swore like a trooper despite a lady being on the footplate. Happy days!

Mr Smith remembers that in June 1983 Archie was again driving No 5051 through Culham station on the down line. By the time he reached Thame Lane Bridge he had set alight all the nearby fields belonging to a local farmer who had a reputation for irascibility. The fire brigade was called and the fire engines squashed all the crops to get to the fires. Instead of suing the railway, the farmer sued the fire brigade!

On 17 March 1991 Archie had No 6024 *King Edward I* on the return run from Derby to Didcot. The inspector was, I think, Clive Rooker (who never drove steam in the steam age – he was far too young) and he told Archie to pass Oxford gently. As they passed the platform end Archie was still doing 30mph, so he got reported and was taken off driving steam locomotives.

A couple of months later I was at Culham station watching 4-6-2 No 71000 *Duke of Gloucester* doing shuttle runs between Didcot and Oxford. I bumped into Colin Postle, who was the Train Planning Officer at Swindon – a very big 'white chief', whom I knew well from my First Aid work at Didcot. He was secretary of our division and I met him many times at competitions (it was he who arranged my two HST footplate trips). Colin asked me which turn was Archie on.

I told him Archie had been suspended, and he said, 'We shall see about that,' and got Archie reinstated!

Archie became a good friend and used to call in on Sundays occasionally with his middle daughter Jacqueline and her son Andrew, aged 5. We had just had our lovely conservatory built, and when Andrew was asked where his Grandad was he replied, 'In the white shed,' pointing to the conservatory! We still call it the 'white shed' 35 years later! Some Sundays I used to go to Archie's for Sunday lunch when his wife Jane was away. He was addicted to garlic and his roast chicken had about a whole bulb in it!

I used to invite Archie and Tony

Archie driving No 5051 *Earl Bathurst*.

Archie makes a tremendous slip at Didcot North Junction. Fireman Tony Neal is hanging out of the cab.

Lyford to my house to watch railway films. However, we would go down to 'The Anchor' for a couple of pints. Pat Ware, a former signalman from East End box, joined us several times. He came in his own car, and was a bit tight with cash, so he would drive around the block three times and arrive just as one of us was buying the first round so he could drink for free. We got fed up with this, so the next time we drove around the block four times and he had to buy all the drinks! Sam Essex, a Didcot driver, joined us once; he told the most amazingly funny, clean jokes you have ever heard, but when he retired he never went to the Staff Club. His brother Peter was a guard who came to our First Aid courses a few times.

When Archie died in August 2010, Colin Postle wrote that he was 'a tremendous character, good railwayman and steam loco driver second to none. Archie, as much if not more than any other I knew, captured

Archie (right) with his fireman, the late Tony Lyford.

the theatre of preserved steam on the main line – marvellous memories.'

Archie's grandson Darren had to clear four sheds full of bike parts; Archie used to mend bikes in his spare time to help supplement his income – they called him the 'Bike Doctor' locally. Darren also found metal tubes full of old railway detonators and some phosphorus flares. He put them online to sell, but the police were called, who then summoned the Didcot Bomb Squad from Vauxhall Barracks, and they undertook a controlled explosion!

I used to give Archie three free medical magazines every week in exchange for *Rail News* – he was very interested in medicine. This started in 1980, and when he died his daughters had to clear 30 years' worth – he had kept them all!

Gone With Regret
L T (Archie) Davies

Born 11 October 1926 in Neath, South Wales, Archie was one of six boys; he married Linda Fisher on 5 October 1946 and they had three daughters.

Archie joined the Railway as a cleaner in Neath in 1943 and later moved to Oxford as a locomotive fireman, before progressing to his work as a driver. He built quite a reputation for driving at speed, of which he was very proud, and his experiences as train driver ranged from standing at the helm of the *Flying Scotsman*, to that of Thomas the Tank Engine! He drove many GWS excursions in the 1980s and 1990s. He retired in 1991 after 48 years of service with the GWR and BR.

Archie was a terrific character and was well known and loved by everyone he met. He was very interested in medicine and greatly valued his friendship with Dr Wayne Smith, who was also a keen railway enthusiast. In fact, Archie loved nothing more than to trade railway memorabilia for medical tips with Wayne, who became the son that Archie never had.

Another of Archie's interests was his love of bike-building. His bicycle always stood out from the crowds, with their multi-coloured mudguard each one a true character, much like himself! He loved trading and bartering with people for bike parts and he loved to mend bikes for friends and acquaintances. His friends would agree that the word bartering was probably created for Archie!

Archie was the original stimulus for the Archie character to be seen all over DRC though the likeness was not too certain! Archie died during the last week of August 2010.

Right: Gone With Regret – the Great Western Society's obituary to Archie was taken mainly from his grandson's eulogy at his funeral.

Below: Harry Merrick at the controls of No 5051 *Earl Bathurst* at Heyford.

Harry Merrick

Harry, one of Didcot's top link drivers, ran over and killed a patient from the mental hospital at Cholsey near Wallingford, who stepped out from behind a bridge support on the railway. Harry was on the verge of retirement but the railway allowed him to return to driving to get his confidence back. He later drove for the Great Western Society at Didcot, working with former fireman Tony Neal and driving No 6998 *Burton Agnes Hall*. In 1973 the author was allowed to operate her on a passenger train, and even though I left the railway in 1966 I never forgot how to drive a locomotive – I could still do it today!

Sadly he developed dementia in the early 1970's and died in 1982. He was another fine man, one of the best, and a great friend to the Kelly family.

Right: Jeanette Howse carries Eccles cakes for a Great Western Society promotional event. Harry Merrick is in the centre.

Below: Harry Merrick with preserved 'Castle' No 7018 *Drysllwyn Castle*.

GWR 'Hall' Class 4-6-0 No 6998
Burton Agnes Hall

The last train to pull out of Oxford station hauled by a steam locomotive at the end of 1965 was *Burton Agnes Hall*, bringing back memories of all the GWR locomotives that had been seen there through the years. She had been cleaned up to head the 2.20pm service to York, but only as far as Banbury. While standing at the down platform the Lord Mayor of Oxford, Alderman Mrs Kathleen Lower, held the regulator. The driver was Gerry Faulkner and the fireman Pat Cook, who had brought the locomotive out of the Oxford depot; also on the footplate was Reginald Hanks, Chairman of the Western Region.

After returning to the shed at Oxford, No 6998 left on the Up Relief line to Didcot, where she was sold direct to the Great Western Society in running order. She initially stayed over at Didcot, then went down to Totnes in April 1966. She left there in 1967 and returned to her new home at Didcot loco shed that December. By 1964 she had travelled some 554,900 miles.

Burton Agnes Hall is located near Driffield in East Yorkshire, a long way from Great Western territory!

Although a Great Western design, No 6998 was built at Swindon Works and completed in the early days of British Railways on 28 January 1949. She cost £8,500 to build, which included her boiler at £2,262. The tender cost an extra £2,035, and was the Hawksworth flat, high-sided design. The total weight was 122t 10cwt and she was 63ft 0¼in long. The firemen did not like the Hawksworth 4,000-gallon tender while running on the main line, so the loco's tenders were changed over the years. In 1951 she received Collett-designed tender No 2647, and other Collett tenders followed in 1954 (No 2914), 1955 (No 2758), 1958 (No 2765), 1961 (No 2394) and 1962 (No 2449). In 1963 Hawksworth tender No 4078 was used.

The locomotive was allocated to Cardiff (1949-58), Shrewsbury (1958-59), Tyseley (1959-60), Fishguard Goodwick (1960-61), Old Oak Common (1961-63), Oxford (1963), Southall (1964-65) and finally Oxford again (1965). She received her final overhaul at Swindon.

No 6998 was named after Burton Agnes Hall, an Elizabethan home near Driffield in East Yorkshire. The house contains many treasures including paintings by Renoir and Gauguin, while the gardens have appeared on television on several occasions, including the maze.

Jack Dearlove

Jack Dearlove was our inspector at Didcot shed – he was dedicated and very good at his job. He knew everything about the workings of the steam locomotive and would not allow anything to get by him, down to every nut and bolt or piece of copper wire.

There were four men who really trained me throughout my apprenticeship during my time at Didcot shed from 1960 to 1965: Inspectors Jack Dearlove and Ted Powell (on shift work), lifting shop fitter Jimmy Tyler, and fitter Jim Holmar, who worked at the front of the shed on repairs.

When any engine came into the shed it had to come down to the ashpit to have the ash and clinker thrown out onto the ground, and the smokebox ash shovelled out. Once the engine was ready to leave the ashpit we got the 'all clear' with thumbs up from the coal stage crew, then Jack and I made our way across to the coal stage to do some of the inspection tasks while there was still steam in the cylinders and boiler. The first job was to put the red 'Not to Be Moved' safety board on the front lamp bracket, then we climbed onto the footplate steps on the tender and wound down the tender hand brake as tight as we could; we both held onto the handle pulling and pushing and locked it down. Next Jack walked along the boiler frame holding the side hand rail with one hand with his lamp in the other to the

A GWR locomotive smokebox. *Frank Dumbleton collection*

front. He undid the smokebox door using the two handles that kept it closed and sealed; turning them anti-clockwise the door opened enough for him to get his fingers into the crack and swing it open wide.

Holding his 'Aladdin' paraffin lamp with its flame exposed, giving off a horrible smell of burning oil, he shouted, 'OK, ready – only one notch and put the vacuum brake on, Pat.'

I did as instructed, applied the vacuum brake and opened the regulator to one notch. The engine wanted to move but nothing happened. I staying on the footplate awaiting orders. Meanwhile Jack climbed into the smokebox; he was in there a while, so I hung over the side waiting to see him come out, then I saw the lamp come out first, and Jack shouted, 'Shut it down!' He beckoned me to join him, and wanted me to climb into the smokebox to show me what he had done. I saw a chalk mark on one of the superheater elements and how he had rubbed off the ash that covered the bend using cotton waste. Jack explained what had happened, with the aid of a small drawing – the engine had no pulling power and was not performing as it should, and inside one of the fire tubes one of the superheater elements had a split in it and was leaking internally. He said he would go back on the footplate and do what I had done, and I had to climb into the smokebox with the smoking lamp and check every superheater element as he had done to see what happened. After a while I saw the flame being drawn into the boiler tube and it nearly sucked the flame out of the lamp. I climbed out onto the frame and waved 'OK.' Jack shut the regulator and I walked along the frame back to the footplate and thanked him for the lesson. I always enjoyed his company and he was a cracking good teacher.

The shed driver now removed the red board and placed it on the footplate, then took the engine to the turntable and turned it 180 degrees. It was then brought back to No 1 road, as we had to do some more inspections. I climbed up onto the footplate and got the red board, again placing it on the rear lamp bracket on the tender.

The next day, waiting for wash-out on No 2 road was No 4959 *Purley Hall*. Jack was holding a pointed iron bar and told me to get under the engine; he passed down the bar and jumped into the pit. We both went under the engine and he took the bar and rammed it under the front frame then, placing it under the Automatic Warning System (AWS) shoe he heaved upwards and we both heard the bell sounding on the footplate. Jack told me to go onto the footplate and reset the system before he pushed up the bar again. I did this several times, then I removed the covering plate and when he pushed the bar up again I could see the workings in operation and the moving of the levers – how the AWS equipment worked together with the small box on the footplate.

GWR 'Hall' Class 4-6-0 No 4959 *Purley Hall*.

I had to go to the stores with a chitty that Jack had signed for a new iron shoe for the AWS. He then showed me how to replace the shoe. We tested it again using same method as before, then when we finished he told me to apply a small amount of thin oil on the levers and replace the cover to the AWS box. Jack asked me to go to the stores again and get a new 'pepper pot' valve for the AWS, as the drivers had a habit of stuffing the valve with paper and other objects to stop the whining noise when it ran over the centre bar between the rails.

Everything Jack found he wrote down in a notebook and later transferred his notes onto the brown inspection sheet, giving the engine number and a list of required repairs.

Working on the footplate he found that the regulator gland was leaking, and noted it down. There wasn't much steam in the boiler, so to save time we both removed the regulator lever. I thought it looked funny when the handle that drove this huge monster was gone. He undid the gland nuts slowly and evenly then, with a small crows-foot iron bar, pulled of the gland. Some steam escaped, but we checked the gauge and carried on anyway and just got on with it. Jack taught me a lot about steam things that people would not attempt – and how easy it was to get really burned.

Down I got again with another chitty to sign for graphite string from the stores, while he raked out the old string. When I came back onto the footplate he was ready to proceed. He re-packed the gland the proper way and replaced the nuts, tightening them evenly; then the regulator was replaced and secured.

'Back underneath, Pat,' but this time I had a scraper with me and some cotton waste dipped in paraffin. Jack started with the trailing wheel on one side, while I started on the leading wheel on the other side, and we both scraped the oily muck off the springs and wiped them over. We were looking for broken springs or a cracked leaf. The muck on our hands was thick and messy, and included the human waste that had come from carriage toilets and had been picked up from the sleepers and spread across the motion underneath the engine. Sometimes we even found human remains. Jack found one spring on the driving wheel that needed attention; wiping his hands he got out his notebook, wrote down the wheel and counted the leaves, wiping the broken one with his cotton waste and marking it with his chalk.

Jack also noted that all the brake blocks needed to be changed, even on the tender; it seemed never-ending, the amount of work that had to be done. However, no other broken spring was found.

Jack told me to get the oilcan and squirt the threads of the screw of the water scoop, while he went onto the footplate and wound it down. I shouted 'OK' and banged the side of the frame with a hammer he had left in the pit, still squirting oil as the screw twirled and the scoop went under the tender into its slot. The last job of the inspection, while he was on the footplate, was to pull all the levers that opened the sand pipes onto the rail; nothing came out, so that went into the

book. Every sand pipe was blocked.

It was coming up to my time to leave for the day and go home at 5.00pm. I carried some of Jack's tools into the lifting shop and placed them in his tool cupboard, having wiped them with paraffin cotton waste and dried them off with clean waste. He then struggled in with the rest of the tools and the iron bar, which I hurriedly took from him. He thanked me, which meant the world to me, even today as I write these memories. Jack Dearlove was the man, and one of the four best men in our Running & Maintenance department at 81E.

Jack had to work a 12-hour shift from 6.00am till 6.00pm, then ride his bicycle home to Blewbury, 5 miles outside Didcot, in all weathers, even snow. When it snowed heavily in 1963 he would leave his home at 3.00am to arrive at the shed for 6.00am, walking all the way pushing his bike along the ruts in the snow on the road where heavy vehicles had passed. He had his lunchbox in his ex-Army canvas bag slung over his shoulder; in those days there was no salt for the roads, so we just had to get on with it. If we were late for work we were stopped money from our wage packets.

An empty locomotive sand box.

The large and heavy driving wheel spring beneath a GWR locomotive.

A driving wheel brake block.

A water scoop, hinged beneath the tender.

The winter of 1963 was particularly severe. John Pritchard took this picture on his way to Woodford Halse with a tender of ovals and dust. He recalls that, 'It was so cold the water froze on the coal and the fire irons were stuck together. *John Pritchard collection*

Another winter 1963 view at Banbury station with a tender full of Midland coal boulders. *John Pritchard collection*

Jimmy Tyler

Next morning I arrived at work and went into the booking area to sign in for work. Mrs Bray gave me my tag, 388, then I walked down to the fitting shop. A lot of brake blocks were stacked together and it seemed that someone was working on an engine changing the brake blocks. The smokebox door was wide open, and there were tools everywhere. As I walked into the locker room to get my overalls out of my lock-up a small face appeared at the door.

'Pat, you're with Jimmy Tyler from today.'

'OK, Arthur, thank you.'

Scrambling into my overalls and walking along at the same time, I found Jimmy at the forge where he was drinking a cup of black tea from his dirty cup.

'You OK, boy?'

'Yes, Jim, ta.'

'We have a big job on today. All the repairs you and Jack found yesterday have got to be done – that's why everyone available and has been put on the "Hall" on road two.'

He finished his tea and slung the dregs into the forge fire, with a spit of steam rising up from the hot coals.

'Right, get the two-wheeled barrow from outside and meet me at the "Hall". I will bring the tools and crowbars, then get yourself up to the stores for a few pounds of cotton waste.' He gave me a chitty that he had signed.

A collection of large spanners in a heritage railway workshop.

I went under the engine with him and he told me to undo the huge nut under the spring hanger. I tried desperately to hold the large spanner under the nut and undo it by tugging on the spanner. Jim chuckled and with his strength gave me a hand – I felt weak and soft as I was only a boy of 15 years old, just out of the boys' school at Didcot.

We removed the nuts from both ends of the springs, then we both crawled out from under the engine and went back into the fitting shop, me pushing the barrow to get the small blocks that were used to jack up heavy items. We placed the hydraulic jack and the blocks on the barrow. Jimmy held the jack firmly while I pushed the barrow back to the pit area. Jim went off and found a pit board and slung it into the pit under the tender, then dragged it into position where we were about to start work. I emptied the barrow on the side of the line and climbed into the pit at the rear of the tender, heaving the timbers into the pit and pulling the hydraulic jack towards me. I lifted the jack and dropped it slowly down, grabbing at the handle until I was confident I could hold its weight in my hands. Then I got down on my knees and crawled along the pit dragging the jack, then the timbers, to where we had to change this spring unit. I made sure to keep my head and shoulders low, as I did not want to crack my head!

The pit board was put into place beneath the centre of the axle with the wooden blocks on top of it; they were dirty, oily, smelly wooden blocks impregnated with years of dirt and oil and chucked about in

all corners of the shed. Jim got out his small tommy bar with a rat's tail, put the small rat's tail into the loop of the split pin and knocked it with his hammer. He told me to do the same on my side. It took a while but he was patient; I got there in the end, and out it came. Happy now – I was coming along.

'Right, I'll go outside and do the same to the centre pin.'

That done the spring was now loose under the axle. He told me to move away under the ashpan area under the engine. Then with his pointed bar he hammered the pins out of the spring hanger and they shot out like bullets. Jim told me to come outside and give him a hand. Doing as I was told, he rammed the iron bar between the wheel spokes and the bottom of the spring, and I stood on the end holding onto the engine frame while he placed the tommy bar on the last centre pin and hit the hammer hard. Out flew the pin but the bar was jammed into the slot, which gave me a jolt as the spring dropped. I pushed down on the bar with my weight, while Jimmy pulled out his bar, then I pulled myself up to the frame and the spring fell off the bar onto the pit board.

We both went back underneath the engine, and Jim told me to keep clear while he manoeuvred the spring with the bar onto the pit floor. He tied a rope around the spring and we both went out into the open pit and pulled the spring out. Lashing another loop on the other end of the spring while I held it, he climbed out of the pit. It seemed no more than a piece of plastic to him, he was so strong. I helped where I could to get it out onto the hard ground.

We placed the spring onto the wheelbarrow and took it outside to the other end of the fitting shop to get the correct size. We counted the leaves of each spring but, sod's law, we had not got one, so Jimmy decided to strip the old spring out with all the leaves and find another old spring. We stripped that one out as well, took out the

Spare locomotive springs.

leaf and measured it against the old one, then replaced it. Using a clamp to hold the spring together, we rebuilt it and took it back to the pit.

Picking up the pins and taking them into the fitting shop, I ground the edges off them on the grindstone, and that gave the leading edge a start within the hole when they were ready to be knocked in. I did the same with the nuts on the studs; we put oil onto the threads and ran the nuts up and down the threads so we would have a free and easy run when putting it all back together.

Then it was tea break at 10.00am in the cabin or mess room.

Next came the hard bit. We put the rope over the ends of the spring and manhandled it down into the pit. At the back of the tender we both started pulling the spring under the engine, keeping our heads low. It then had to be lifted up onto the pit board. God, this is going to be heavy! I put the rope over the centre of the axle and Jimmy made a loop and tied it off into the spring eye. As I pulled on the rope Jimmy lifted the spring straight up and slung it onto the pit board. I looked at him and the sweat was running down his face – what a man and a half!

He wiped his face with clean cotton waste, then we both turned the spring into the upright position. By jamming a bar into the holes at each end of the spring and pressing and lifting we accomplished it. Placing a wooden block on the pit board, we manoeuvred the spring unit onto it and into a position from where it could be raised upwards so the pins could be knocked in. Jimmy went outside with the long bar and placed it between the spokes of the wheel. I pushed the spring downwards so the end went up. At this stage one of the other fitters, Jimmy Holmar, came underneath and between them the two men got the spring back into position, hung it, placed the pins back into the slots, and helped to finish the job.

We carried all the items back to the fitting shop, washed our hands and dried them with cotton waste, then went back to help out where we could with the other men working on the engine.

Jimmy said we would now change a superheater, and told me get a cloth and wrap it around my neck, do up my overalls to my neck and tie off the ends of my overall cuffs so that no soot would get into my clean clothes. 'Do as I am doing, Pat.' I put a cap on my head, and we went to get the tools and oilcan with a mix of oils and paraffin. We knew which superheater element it was that was leaking, so I was given a wire brush and had to scrape the rust off the nuts. Jim passed the oilcan to me and I squirted the nuts and threads. Then he passed in a socket spanner with an iron bar attached – these were not the nice shiny sockets of today, but old ones that had been about at that time of Noah's Ark! With the iron bar rammed into the hole on the end of the socket, we both heaved off the nuts – then I knew what the fuss was about regarding screaming nuts on a rusted dried thread. It brought tears to my eyes and hurt my ears! Then we worked on the other one – same idea and same screaming noise. We were lucky – someone must have been helping us from far away in the land of dead engines – for the nuts came off with a spanner, helping by oil squirted on the threads.

As we pulled out the superheater from its holding tube I had never ever seen anything like it – it just kept coming and coming. Suddenly the end emerged and Jim lifted it up in the air and pulled it while I grabbed it as it fell out of the tube. I sat on the blastpipe with a piece of wood across the hole, sitting on cotton waste, and handed the superheater down to Jim on the ground.

He waited for me to climb down and led the way into the fitting shop and out to where the springs were kept, but this time we went into a little corrugated-tin shed with the superheater and measured it up against another one of the same size, 15 feet long. I was told to go back and clean down the threads and oil them, try the nuts over the threads and check that they ran freely with help from a spanner.

When I had done this I went back in to help Jimmy carry the superheater back to the engine. I climbed up into the smokebox and he handed the heater end up as I started to find the hole to fit it back into position. I looked around and Jimmy was there pushing the new superheater back into the long tube until near the end when we took a new graphite gasket and fitted it into position, so that the studs ran through the holes on the joint on the superheater. Then the nuts were tightened down very tight.

There was still more work to do, but Jimmy said that we had done enough. But we were a dedicated few.

Working the forge

While laying half asleep early one morning recently, now retired for the last ten years, I got to thinking about those times long passed in 1960 when I was a young boy of 15 years old, experiencing the excitement and romance of my first job working for British Railways as a fitter's boy. I was not old enough to start my apprenticeship until the following year, February 1961, when I could start my proper career.

In my imagination I ran my hands once more over the engine frames and all the rivets that were used to secure the frames together, thinking about the men that worked in those great factories of Swindon and Old Oak Common, hammering and working with rivet hammers, rounding the heads. There the raw metal started to turn into something that looked like a steam locomotive, the locomotives I fell in love with, the 'Halls', the pannier tanks and the 'Moguls.'

I remember working in Didcot shed, climbing over the steam engines, being a little cocky and sometimes a bit too clever. Sometimes I felt I was back at school – don't get me wrong, I really enjoyed being at school, those were the best years of my life. But at the same time I couldn't wait to start my new career, working for British Railways.

I remember the way I was taught to do things the proper way, how to handle the metal files and, most importantly, how to use them to work the rough edges from a piece of metal, making the shape that was required. There were different kinds of files with different cutting edges, smooth, fine and bastard (meaning a very rough file). The art of finding how to bring something that was rusty with indented edges back to life was something to be proud of.

There were other tools that were going to be needed to proceed in my future career before I would be a fully fledged apprentice fitter and turner. I had started to find old files from the scrap areas around the site, thrown under and between the sleepers and the grass verges, and collected them up and took them to the forge area. There I was shown how to stoke up the fire, but it was the same principle as when I worked in the metal shop at school. Blacksmithing was something I really enjoyed – the only difference was the blower controls. At the forge I was given a wire brush, and placed it on the anvil ready to be used.

I placed the old files into the burning forge fire with the blower raging and sparks exploding outwards from the old coals, then raked new coals over into the burning area to help burn the years of dust and dirt from the rough edges. I took a pair of long-handled pliers from the rack, squeezing the handles together after I had placed them over the file end, and removed it from forge onto the flat top of the anvil. Then the wire brush came into use. Still holding the file in the pliers in my left hand, with the wire brush in my right hand I scrubbed over the file with some force, the lumps of dirt blowing away and the file left ready to be worked on.

With a 2½lb BR(W) ball-headed hammer and the file glowing crimson, I brought the hammer down onto it. The magic was just about to start: the half-round 10-by-1-inch long-handled file was taking shape slowly. I placed it back into the forge with the blower still on the fire, then pulled it out and tempered it by slowly dipping it in water, watching the water bubbling and turning to steam, as if it was screaming to me to hit the file again and again as it took shape. I finally doused it into the water trough slowly, and it was finished. Turning off the blower, I pulled the grindstone goggles down over my head. The grindstone was run off a belt system from a huge motor – the fitters saw to that, it was new to me.

The old-fashioned grinder thumped and groaned as it went round and round – there were no guards to protect this big rough-looking 12-inch-diameter wheel. It frightened me really to attempt to start grinding, placing the file onto the wheel with sparks starting to scatter off it. But it encouraged to keep going and prove that I could do this. All the rough edges had been removed after a few moments. I had a look at it – just a little more and it would be done. I was completely chuffed when it went into action a few days later, scrapping out a white-metal bushing that had been made in the same forge that I had worked at.

All these years later I got up and went out to find my toolbox in the garage, and found the tools that I had made all those years back, still together, nearly 60 years later.

Fitters

At Didcot shed the Running & Maintenance staff kept up with most of the engineering problems that arose. The only thing that I never saw was a boiler being removed from its frame. No locomotive ever went to Swindon for fitting work, only for boiler and tube replacements or modifications – all the other engineering work was carried out within our shed. During those years our dedication was to BR – home life came second.

Fitter Bob Looms worked within the shed doing planned maintenance work or changing brake blocks on locos or tenders with either an apprentice who was free or the fitter's mate, Bob Warrick. Bob Looms had been born in Belgium and got out of the country before the Germans invaded; he came to England and joined the RAF, and when he walked into the shed he was really smartly dressed in nice brown shoes and grey

flannels and a blue jacket with the crest of the RAF on his pocket – he was so proud. Fitter Bert Passey either helped Bob Looms do a 12,000-mile planned maintenance or one of the easy ones with apprentice Bengy Carter.

From left to right, Matt Oglesby, Bert Passey and Bob Looms. *Author's collection*

Fitter Dave Davis with his fitter's mate. Jim Hale carried out 15,000-mile planned maintenance work, which took two or three days to complete. When required they would help Jimmy Tyler and myself in the fitting shop stripping out locomotives.

Fitter Ted Powell and his fitter's mate Frank Dowding were on inspections as the engines came in off the main line and had their fires dropped. They worked over at the coal stage before the engine went down to the turntable.

Fitter Jimmy Holmar and his fitter's mate Matt Oglesby would be out at the front of the shed completing the repairing of faults on locomotives ready to leave on all four roads. They might need replacement of a broken boiler gauge glass or adjustments to the vacuum brakes, the sand pipes or the tender brakes. The Shed Foremen on duty

were Bernard Barlow, Harry Buckle or Reg
Warr, strutting up and down with their
bowler hats on, trying to get the engines out
on time.

Fitter Jack Dearlove worked on
inspections and was a tip-top dedicated
railwayman – he would never allow anything
to get past him. In 1965 I once saw him get
angry with an Indian fitter that came to
work in our department. His name was Ali
Patel and he kept saying, 'In my country we
do this' or 'In my country we do that.' Jack
had been out in India during the Second
World War and saw many things, including
the filth and dirt. Jack told him to shut his
mouth, but he didn't. Jack got violently
angry, grabbed Ali, dragged him out through
the cabin door and threw him in the pit.

Ali came to work wearing flat leather
flip-flops on his feet and no socks, and he
wore an 'Aladdin'-style overshirt and baggy
pants as if he was still in India – this did not
go down very well with the rest of the fitting
crew. He was told by our Foreman Arthur
Brinkley to get heavy boots and overalls on a
bit quick!

One day in the lifting shop, workshop
fitter Jimmy Tyler and myself were working
on No 6953 *Leighton Hall*. We pushed its
tender outside with help from the rest of
the staff, using crowbars jammed under the
wheels and heaving against the buffers.
We then removed the crosshead from the
locomotive's piston rod, then the outside
connecting rods, side rods, brake blocks and
their connecting rods on both sides of the
engine. This gave easy access to the axle
springs. Undoing the main nuts that held
them, we both lifted off the springs using
our hands and crowbars. Then we undid
the heavy studs that held the axle boxes
together. I climbed under the boiler with a
spanner to hold the bolt head and Jimmy
undid the nut. The axle box was very heavy
and for safety reasons we placed a block
of wood on a plank across the pit before
allowed the bottom of the axle block to drop
off by pulling it with a crowbar.

We next placed the huge heavy hooks

Reg Warr, Shed Foreman (left), with Jimmy Tyler.
Author's collection

A GWR loco crosshead.

on the end of the chains from the crane
under the footplate on either side of the
'Hall'. The stationary fitting shop crane had
been installed by Royce of Manchester in
1932, and it had a 50-ton maximum lift.
Jimmy controlled the operation of the crane
and I held the chains apart with help from
Dave Davis until the hooks went tight,
then I moved away and watched the engine

smokebox go up into the air, with the engine rolling slightly backwards as it was lifted.

The shout went out 'That's enough!' there now being just enough height to roll out the driving wheel clear of the engine, and block it with wood on either side. Then Jimmy operated the crane to lower the engine back down onto the rails. The wooden shed doors had to be opened and all the Running & Maintenance crew manhandled the engine back to the tender, and it was blocked on all wheels.

Within the hour No 1 road had to be

it. We did the same with the axle boxes, securing them with the wheels in the wagon. The next job was the paperwork for Swindon Works, where new tyres would be fitted to the wheels and the axle boxes rebushed. The 'tanky' drew the wagon out to the marshalling yard.

Over the years our fitters worked on steam engines from other sheds and 'foreign' regions. We also looked after single-car diesel multiple units and diesel shunters, including Paxmans.

A pair of driving wheels in the workshop. *R. J. Russell collection*

cleared of all engines so that a 'tanky' could be brought into the fitting shop with an empty open wagon. Jimmy and I placed the lifting bar through the spokes of the wheel set and hooked it up to the crane, lifting the wheels into the air. Then a couple of us pushed an open wagon under the crane, put the brake on and lowered the wheels into

Locomotives allocated to Didcot shed (81E) in 1960

Nos 1502, 2201, 2221, 2230, 2240, 2819, 2836, 2839, 2849, 3211, 3211, 3622, 3653, 3751, 4649, 4902, 4915, 4939, 4950, 4959, 4965, 4969, 4976, 5351, 5380, 5746, 5918, 5943, 5987, 6109, 6113, 6124, 6136, 6139, 6156, 6159, 6302, 6313, 6363, 6379, 6910, 6915, 6937, 6953, 6969, 6983, 7324, 7327, 8720.

Stefan

No record of railway operations around Didcot would be complete without a mention of a very important man rarely seen by the public – the signal lamp man. The lamp man in our district was a Polish chap called Stefan, the most cheerful little person imaginable, although he had one of the roughest jobs on the Western Region. In all weathers he would start going round the district each week beginning at Milton. The signalmen would know he was about because the copper wire coil in the signal lamps would contact when he took out the lamp, causing a low-voltage current to ring the 'Lamp Out' warning bell in the signal box. He would trim and fill the lamps in the small tin lamp hut near each box, then trudge off with his lamp stick, carried on his shoulder, loaded down with a dozen lamps suspended from it, all filled with long-burning oil.

Stefan had to climb up tall signal posts while gale-force winds blew, hanging on for dear life, or on rainy days getting wet though to his underwear, but he wouldn't moan. Milton to Foxhall Junction would be a day's work, but East Junction would take him all day from early morning till late evening. As well as the lamps on signal posts he also had to refill the ground signals. He kept his head down and worked away happily, his week's work ending at Sandford, north of Radley. He then started back at Milton the following Monday morning, whatever the weather, and all the signalman would hear him singing happily in Polish. One signalman asked him where he came from, and Stefan said he had suffered a few years being hungry and cold, and had worked as a slave on fortifications in France and Germany during the war, but had survived going back and forth across Europe.

He worked overtime on Sundays supplying signal boxes with coal from a wagon filled at Didcot shed, coupled to a guard's van and pulled by a pannier tank. They called at each signal box, replenishing the coal stocks. He also placed a barrel of oil in the storage compartment under the signal box, which he used to top up the lamps. The coal was loaded at the shed either by Stefan or the shed labourer, sometimes with help from Lewis Holmar, Jimmy Holmar's son, if he was visiting the shed. Stefan left enough supplies at each box for six months.

In 1965 Stefan went missing from the shed and the signalling department for a couple of days and no one knew where he was. Someone walking round the lake by the Provender Stores one Sunday morning found a stack of clothes folded neatly on the ground near the water's edge. He ran across the rails to the shed, and Jimmy Holmar grabbed a hook and rope and went back with a few other men and dragged the lake, but found nothing. Stefan had gone with the two children and two other men from the railway who had committed suicide back in the 1950s.

Chapter 4
Reading shed, 81D

All out!

Working on steam engines for British Railways could be the hardest career that anybody could imagine, with dirt and grime every hour of every day. However, times could change for a young apprentice if he trained as a fitter and tried to gain turning experience, if he was lucky enough to have a decent lathe in the fitting shop – not like the ones we had in our workshop at Didcot. But to my surprise Reading, Oxford and most Western Region systems were all the same, it seems.

The Western Region went on strike on Wednesday 3 October 1962, and all railwaymen except apprentices had to come out. So we had to go through the picket line at the entrance to the station at Didcot. When I came down Station Road it was quiet, no traffic on the road, no one walking about – it was like a ghost town. Also there was no traffic on the railway, no movement anywhere with no Great Western whistles blowing.

I rode my pushbike into the station entrance by the taxi rank. Men were standing in a line dressed in their civilian clothes and arms linked together. I noticed a slight gap in the line that I could ride my bike through, which I thought would be a good idea at the time. One of the men walked up to me, pulled me off my bike and asked me where I was going. One of the fitter's mates from Didcot shed, Jim Hale, pulled the chap off me and said that I was an apprentice and he should leave me alone. The man said sorry to me, and I accepted his apology.

There was one other apprentice from our shed, Bengy, to come through, as well as four or five more for Reading depot, Mick Russell, Dennis Tyler, Mick Massey from Moreton and one called Noddy from Hendred (whose real name was Derek Dawson). That day we all had to be at Didcot shed, so we swept and cleaned out the workshop. We also cleaned the breakdown van and had our lunch in it and read the 'MPII', the Maintenance Inventories, God's handbook for the railway. We went home early in the afternoon.

In the next day's *Daily Sketch* newspaper it was reported that an apprentice from another depot thought he would be clever and take a 150-ton diesel engine home from the area where he was stationed. However, although the whole of the network was on strike, even the signalmen, he didn't think about the catch points, and they found the diesel engine on its side near a signal box – the lad had legged it!

The Labour Club in Didcot was the branch headquarters for the union and the railwaymen who were on strike. They got paid 10 shillings a day, for one day only. Didcot got hit the hardest during the strike.

Reading apprentices

Mick Russell remembers travelling from Didcot to Reading. 'I lived in Sinodun Road, Didcot, and we would catch the 7.05am stopper to Reading as I was an apprentice electrician in the diesel depot. All craftsmen carried keys to open carriage doors – they were a cross-type metal instrument that fitted into a square hole in the door – and some mornings all the apprentices from our area with Hendred and Moreton positioned ourselves in the carriage, then I would lower the window, insert the key, lock the door from the outside, pull the window back up and lock it with the leather strap. When the train stopped at every station to Reading, passengers would try and open our door but to no avail, tugging on the brass handle and trying desperately to get into the carriage (remember that these carriages had no

Above: The approach to Reading shed from the main line. The shed was built in the same style as Didcot, within a triangle of railway lines; both sheds sat in the middle and both fitting shops were of the same design. *Bob Judge collection*

Right: The turntable outside the main shed. *Bob Judge collection*

Below: The fitting shop is seen on the left behind No 5018 *St Mawes Castle. Bob Judge collection*

Reading shed's coal stage. *Bob Judge collection*

Reading steam fitters in the 1960s. From the right they are Ernie Kirk, fitter, Fred Stemp, fitter's mate, and Peter Stringer, fitter. I cannot remember the name of the gentleman on the left. *Bob Judge collection*

Sitting on the tool box is a young Allan Brown, and looking out are Brian Wheeler and Jack Fitzgerald; the latter was a fitter's mate, who worked mainly on 3-5 and 7-9 exams, involving steam valves, injectors and clacks. The locomotive is 'Castle' No 5073 *Blenheim*. *Bob Judge collection*

The foreman, Mr W. Miles, had the bright idea of doing it with hand hydraulic jacks and packing. As we would have to lift about 5 feet, this took a lot of packing. In fact, the breakdown van was now empty. It was a bit scary having the tender that high, especially when "The Bristolian" went by at about 80mph two tracks away. I don't think Health and Safety would have been impressed that day. But the job got done.

'One of the regular jobs was leaking levelling pipes on "61xx" tank locos – these connected and levelled up the water in the two tanks. To access the bolts you had to get into the side tanks via the filler opening – this was a job for a lean apprentice. The only means of illumination was a paraffin lamp – a 'smokey Joe'. It was dark and damp, and the bottom was covered in sludge. The water at Reading was hard, even though we had a water-softening plant. So you crawled to the back and got as comfortable as was possible. By this time word had got around and other apprentices had great pleasure in banging on the side of the tank. The bolt and nuts were of poor quality; the bolts were called "rough" and the nuts "black". The seal was made with hemp string, which you prepared before going into the tank. You just prayed you had done a good job and on filling there would be no leaks. If so, it was drain down again and go back inside.'

The 'bunk'

Reading had several small engines that ran on the rural branch lines in what was then Berkshire (in 1974 the county boundaries were changed, but everyone born before that year, like myself, always proudly claimed to be 'Berkshire born and Berkshire bred', as was the saying at the time). These little trains became popularly known as the 'bunk'.

One was the Abingdon 'bunk', operating on the rural branch between the sleepy stations of Radley and Abingdon, near Oxford.

Early one Friday morning 0-4-2T No 1420 went out from Didcot shed bound for Abingdon. Travelling light engine, the bunker was filled to capacity and there was not much room to move as the fireman fed the firebox with coal. They had to get her to Radley quickly and off the main line to allow the normal passenger and freight trains to pass.

Getting near the junction at Radley, the driver of the 'bunk' pulled the whistle chain to notify the signalman that they are not far away, which gave him time to change the points to allow them into the branch and get

An Oxfordshire 'bunk'. This is Wallingford station, terminus of a short branch from Cholsey & Moulsford on the Great Western main line. The loco is 0-4-2T No 1407 of the same class as No 1420 that worked the Abingdon branch.

them off the main line to Oxford.

The signalman opened his signal box sash window and waved to the enginemen; the signal was 'off', giving clearance for the 'bunk' to proceed on its journey to Abingdon station, still as a light engine, as the coach was waiting in the siding there for them to couple up. After they had passed, the signalman set the points back to normal for the main line and put the 'board' back to the stop position.

The driver of the 'bunk' started to gather speed along this lonely, rural branch railway, not really worried about what might be ahead and the regulator wide open. The fireman was still shovelling coal into the firebox and operating the blower to help bring the steam pressure up. After a few minutes he looked out of the cab's side window as they sped past the hedgerows with not a care in the world. Then suddenly the 'bunk' hit a herd of 20 cows head-on that had wandered onto the line. The milk from several udders splashed over the front of the smokebox doors and the front glass windows, making one hell of a mess, while the animals themselves were cut to pieces by the engine – there were bits of cow everywhere.

The fireman wound the handbrake down and the brakes ground on the tyres. Meanwhile the driver immediately shut the regulator and applied the vacuum brake, but it was a few moments before they were finally able to bring the engine to a stand. They looked out at the carnage, with cattle dead and dying, and those that were able trying to escape.

The crew climbed down onto the cinder path and looked at the appalling state of the area –it was total carnage, with blood and carcases making the scene look more like an abattoir than a railway line. The driver asked the fireman to run ahead to Abingdon station and report what had happened to the station master and instruct him to close the station to passengers. He also notified the signalman at Radley and contacted Didcot shed for instructions. Didcot returned the call and said to go back to the shed at

once. Meanwhile the surviving cattle were rounded up and put back into the field; a gate had been left wide open by someone who had gone through earlier that day and not shut it.

I remember going into the shed that Friday morning to find at the doorway of No 4 road a '14xx' Class 0-4-2T. She was covered in milk and blood and bits of cow, all over the leading end, buffers, smokebox, boiler and cab – it was not a pleasant sight to see. The next time I saw the locomotive she had been cleaned down. The driver and fireman had to put in their reports.

Only rarely did the Abingdon fireman get a shift with his Oxford driver to run on the main line, firing a huge Great Western monster of a locomotive pulling 11 heavy coaches full of passengers from Oxford station. This was far harder work, ensuring that there was enough steam to get them and their train to Paddington station on time; sweat would be dripping from his forehead and down his back from the roaring fire every time he placed a shovelful of coal in the firebox. There was also the effort of raking back the ashes and clinker within the burning mass of coals to make a bed for the fresh coal, making a note of where he placed each shovelful in the box, while the driver opened and shut the firehole door to keep the heat in the firebox.

On arrival at Paddington the locomotive had to run into Ranelagh Yard to be refreshed with coal and water, and the fireman had help from his driver (unlike some Didcot drivers who simply looked on while their fireman did all the work, such as filling the tender with water – the fireman had to get down off the tender and open the valve while the driver did nothing, impatient to be off with his train). The weary Abingdon fireman then helped his driver to take the engine onto the turntable and turn it, before running slowly back into their slot near the block of flats that overlooked the yard. The driver blew the Great Western whistle to say he was there, but although drivers were used to some old women throwing milk bottles down on the engine crews in protest, this was a new thing – the women in the flats above Ranelagh Yard started to empty their chamber pots on the engine crews!

Charlie Caulkett

The late Charlie Caulkett told me that the footplate work at Reading shed gave him lots of main-line work to Weymouth, Taunton and Exeter via the Berks & Hants line to the West Country, and to Worcester and Birmingham Snow Hill. He also worked on the Henley branch, and to Guildford and Redhill. The Marlow branch line was another job, with wonderful sights, before steam came to a end between 1964 and 1966.

'Railwaymen were scrambling for jobs,' he remembered, 'and I had to come off the footplate. I obtained a Goods Guard vacancy at Reading. We had quite a lot of Westbury work and Severn Tunnel jobs, then out of

Special train 'The Sulzer Bagpipe' behind No 33116 travels along Weymouth quay with its two railwaymen escorts. *Neil Harvey collection*

the blue things started to slow down and dwindle away in the early 1970s.

'In 1974 I took up a vacancy at Didcot yard shunting mainly passenger trains. Each night shift we used to shunt about eight trains and also make up trains for the following dayshift ready for when they came on duty.

'I next transferred from the Western Region to the Southern Region at Weymouth depot. My wife did not want to go to Weymouth, but I settled in there straight away. The work was good and the staff very pleasant. I had to start as a Leading Railman, and became the junior man at that depot because it was an inter-regional transfer.

'We were very busy with three boat trains a day to the quay station, which was along a tramway. We met the trains at the junction while the crews changed, then we had to walk though the town in front of the train with two shunters carrying red flags. The Weymouth boat train usually comprised a Class 33 "Crompton" diesel and ten coaches, which included a buffet or dining car.

'We took the train to Weymouth quay

The same train, now with No 33103 leading, returns along the quay with passengers for Waterloo. *Neil Harvey collection*

station, which was about three-quarters of a mile away. On arrival at the quay we got the "Crompton" off, and the engine crew crossing her over by the crossover and reversed her back onto the leading coach; then we coupled her up to the front to form the next up boat train.

'My mate and I had to water and clean the passenger coaches, and clean the inside corridors and seats, collect all the rubbish in bags and place it in the dumper near the tankers. We also had to clean down the diesel engine. Once the Jersey boat had docked and the passengers had disembarked onto the quay and been cleared through customs, we took the train back up the tramway, still walking in front of it to make sure no car was left fouling the tramway lines, slowly proceeding to the junction where a crew of either Waterloo or Weymouth men would work the boat train up to London.

'The last boat train to the quay was at about 22.30, and the passengers would board the last Jersey boat, which sailed from Weymouth quay at 23.00. We again cleaned and watered the passenger coaches, which stood on the quay overnight and formed

the first up Weymouth to Waterloo train at 08.30 the next morning, which was worked by Weymouth men as far as Southampton.

'The work on Sundays at Weymouth was very busy – some days we could get six excursions, and it was shorter day.

'We also used to do two days lamping, checking all the semaphore signal lamps and ground signal lamps from Weymouth to Radipole Halt.

'In the early 1970s the Bridport branch from Maiden Newton was still running. There were two drivers and guards based at Bridport and several Weymouth crews to work other trains. I worked several turns along the branch.

'We had two days of quay work taking down the boat trains, and two days shunting and platform duties, with nine Bristol trains daily worked by Westbury and Bristol men. There was an hourly service to Waterloo, with three boat trains and a Royal Mail train, which was a Travelling Post Office; this train left at about 21.00 to Waterloo.

'I did this for about four years, then a vacancy came up at BR's Shipping Services at Weymouth quay station. I was successful and was put on refuelling and watering duties for the ships at Weymouth. We had five ships to refuel daily – the *Caesarea*, *Sarnia*, *Maid of Kent*, *Earl Harold* and *Earl Godwin* – with two bunker tanks. There was also a German ship that brought in tomatoes from Jersey. The skipper's name was Eodie – he was also German.

'I was bunkering ships from 06.00 to 23.00 in the summer. I had *Maid of Kent* on the Cherbourg run first, then *Earl Harold* as the first Jersey boat. I also had to bunker the Jersey tomato boat. We were allowed to go home for breakfast; I lived near the quay so I used to cycle home and did a bit of gardening for a couple of hours. I used to cycle home three times a day.

'My last ship of the day was *Maid of Kent*, which was a heavy oil burner. I used to pump in the oil from one of the 12 oil tankers from Fawley Terminal; she used 18 tons of HFO (heavy fuel oil) per trip.

'We then helped with the counting of passengers or ticket checks and I used to get home about 23.00pm. We did this all summer – three Jersey boats and two Cherbourg boats. I also had to drive the British Railways launch, the boat that was used to collect the fitters and carpenters for

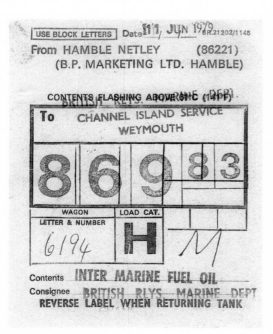

A heavy fuel oil ticket from one of the Weymouth tank wagons. *Charlie Caulkett collection*

the ships, as we had a large workshop and a slipway next to the lifeboat station. I had also to learn to use the dock cranes, of which there were five at Weymouth quay.

'I did bunkering duties until 1987, when overnight we were made redundant. We were paid off and not allowed to apply for a vacancy on British Railways for three months. If I had applied for a job within that time I would have had to pay back my redundancy.

'I was eventually offered a Ticket Collector's job on the trains. This was a nice little position, assisting the guard on the Bristol to Weymouth and Weymouth to Waterloo passenger trains. After nine months I was promoted to guard on the Waterloo service, as well as the Brockenhurst branch line. Weymouth to Bristol via Yeovil Pen Mill and to Exeter and Cardiff might be a typical day's work. The next day would be Weymouth to Bristol, Bristol to Warminster and back to Bristol, work the Bristol-Weymouth service home, then work the Weymouth to Westbury, then to Bristol, and Bristol to Weymouth. On a Sunday it might be Weymouth to Cardiff and return. For a time we used to work with a Class 37 diesel pulling ten coaches between Weymouth quay and Bristol.

'In 1990 the depot was split up. Five guards went to the Western Region and 15 stayed on the Southern. I chose to go to the Western Region and we came under Westbury depot. Joe Winter was our Guards Inspector; I got on well as I was an ex-Western footplateman and knew what was expected of me.

'This arrangement at Weymouth remained until my retirement in 2001. I retired at Westbury, but first I had to work the Cardiff passenger train to Weymouth. On the day I finished at Westbury I completed 49 years and 2 months of service, with only a short break. I was photographed for *The Railway Magazine*, and that was the end of my service on British Railways, a job that I loved and was sorry when it came to an end.'

Chapter 5
The Lend-Lease programme

During 1942 the SS *Alco* sailed to Britain from the USA bringing steam locomotives as part of the Lend-Lease programme, as insufficient engines were being built here to cope with the war effort. The ships brought in 50 locomotives every month from the big three companies in the United States – Alco, Baldwin and Lima. The engines on the deck were strapped down with their big side rods removed to help when their lowering onto railway lines on the quay. They then travelled to their holding areas, at depots in Ebbw Vale, South Wales, and Southampton for the depot at Eastleigh. Their motions were replaced and they were put through a vigorous inspection by their own Army personnel, the US Army Transportation Corps (USATC). They were then towed to Swindon factory to have modifications made under the standard regulations, and to have their vacuum brakes and tender brakes checked over by British railway personnel. They had ash pan hoods fitted (the firebox temperatures reached more than 3,000 degrees F on test) before being allowed to travel in the British Isles.

Reading was allocated one USATC 'S160' 2-8-0 loco, and Didcot received three.

This and previous page: USATC 'S160' 2-8-0 locos are lifted off the deck of SS *Alco*, with their lettering and numbers painted over to prevent them being identified by German U-boats. Some of the locos' motion and some wheel sets have been removed, to be refitted once the engines are on dry land.

At Reading West marshalling yard on 14 September 1943 'S160' No 2054, with its crew, guard and a shunter, shunts wagons and box vans to make up a train.

Top: With a permanent way gang looking on, No 2054 passes Reading with a freight train. *R. J. Russell collection*

Above: With its safety blowing off, Reading's 'S160' runs along the main line with a freight. (When safety valves blew off like this within a station the canopy got a steam clean to remove many years of dirt and grime!)

Chapter 6
The Polar Star

The Polar Star hostel at Didcot.

Railway hostels played a crucial part in the staffing of the Western Region. Didcot's hostel was built at the beginning of the Second World War to accommodate railwaymen from all parts of the GWR area. The hostel was built on the 'H block' design with accommodation for more than 100 men together with the staff who manned the 24-hour canteen and looked after the general running of the building for the sum of 7 shillings per week. As well as the canteen, there was a games room with a full-size snooker table, a TV room, laundry facilities,

Former driver John Pritchard stands outside the hostel many years later. He lived here from 1961 to 1965 after moving to Didcot from South Wales as a novice fireman. *John Pritchard collection*

The 'Residents Entrance' to Polar Star.

'Among some of the characters was Stan Pritchard (not a relative), a passed fireman who came to Didcot in the early 1960s from South Wales. He was quite normal until he had a few drinks, then he became unpredictable. On one occasion I was in the canteen at about 10.00pm; the room was empty except for myself and the old porter who was mopping the floor, when all of a sudden the double doors flew open and Stan led a horse into the room. He was feeding it lumps of sugar. He said it had followed him home. The horse got to the centre of the canteen then lifted his tail and let go everything. The mess and stink was horrendous as the horse tramped all its droppings across the floor. The old porter went berserk. However, Stan said, "I'm taking the horse to my room," and led it towards the stairs. However, the horse

bathrooms, a clothes drying room, and the 24-hour call board manned by the hostel porter. The very small single rooms had just enough space for a bed, a narrow wardrobe and a two-drawer chest; a 4-inch heating pipe ran through each room, and the light was a naked 40-watt bulb. The walls were breeze blocks painted a cream colour.

Above the entrance to the hostel was the 'Polar Star' nameplate from No 4005, a Churchward 'Star' Class locomotive that had been withdrawn from service at Old Oak Common in 1934.

It was very basic but would be John Pritchard's home until the end of steam in 1965 and the end of his railway career. 'I arrived at the hostel in the spring of 1961 as a 16-year-old novice fireman suddenly thrust into a man's world. Some of my old Didcot acquaintances have criticised me for committing my experiences and memoirs to paper because of my relatively short railway career, compared with their 40 to 50 years, yet when the author of this book gave them the opportunity to add their own experiences the silence was deafening!

John Pritchard, 16 years old in 1961, stands on the wasteland at the back of the hostel, in the company of stabled DMUs. *John Pritchard collection*

refused to climb them.

'The porter had called the police, but luckily by the time they arrived Stan and the horse had disappeared. They asked me what had happened and I said a horse had walked into the canteen. No further action was taken.

'Stan's drinking problem got worse and it began to be noticed by the Loco Department management, and he was eventually spoken to and took offence. I did not witness his last day at Didcot but Shady Johns, a very good friend of mine, did. They were both in the booking hall in the shed, and Stan and the foreman were having words. The foreman eventually said to Stan, "If you wish to resign then put it in writing."

'Stan grabbed a piece of paper and wrote in 6-inch letters, "I QUIT!"

'He was never seen again.

'At the rear of the hostel was a large area of wasteland of about an acre or more, and on it stood a derelict single-storey building that had once been used as a sports facility for boxing (of which more later). A few of us young firemen decided to explore it, just for something to do. One lad noticed that the old light fittings in the main hall were hanging down from the ceiling, and they were made of brass.

'He said, "If we collect them we might be able to sell then for scrap."

'I said, "What if the power is still on?"

'He said, "Don't be daft!" and stuck his fingers in the socket fitting to prove it. Suddenly he started to leap about and scream. We thought he was messing about and joined in the performance. Then we noticed he was turning a funny colour. One of the lads found the switch and turned the power off. The clown sat on the floor for a few moments while he recovered. The rest of us were holding our aching sides and wiping tears from our eyes. It was no laughing matter for the victim, but for us boys it was a hilarious.

'On another occasion a few of the lads decided to turn the wasteland behind the hostel into a scramble track complete with jumps and a water dip. An old BSA Bantam 125cc bike was purchased for a few pounds and the track was open for business. We all had a go and some of us actually learned to ride a motorcycle during that time. Training to ride was pretty basic – sit on the saddle of the bike, pull in the clutch lever, engage the gear, rev the engine and let out the clutch lever. To stop, pull in the clutch and stamp on the foot brake, putting the gear in neutral.

'Cyril, a young fireman from the West Country, decided to have a go. He was shown the procedure, and we all watched him rev the bike to absolute maximum. He let out the clutch and shot down the track through the water dip, almost disappearing in the splash. By now he was screaming. With both his legs off the foot pegs and pointing forward like two ramrods, he then hit the jump at about 25mph and took

Shady Johns sits on John Pritchard's motor bike on the area of wasteland. In the background is East Junction signal box. *John Pritchard collection*

off. We all cheered. "Go for it, Cyril!" He managed to land safely but just kept on going into a concrete fence post, snapping it in two and breaking his left leg in the process.

'After that incident the hostel manager decided to close the track.

'Many young firemen came to Didcot from parts of the Western Region that were in areas of high unemployment. I myself came from South Wales, and others came from the West Country. I guess today we would call them economic migrants. Many eventually married and settled in Didcot. One example was Antony Groves, who

The Polar Star nameplate, sold at auction in 2012 for £22,500.

came to the hostel in 1962 from Truro in Cornwall. We became friends and still keep in touch. Many lasting friendships were made and many more lost when the hostel finally closed and we all went our separate ways.'

Finally, regarding the 'Polar Star' nameplate, it was claimed that after the hostel closed a local driver borrowed it by putting a ladder to the building, though there were no witnesses. About four years ago I was browsing an auction site on the Internet and to my surprise saw that the 'Polar Star' nameplate had just been sold. The write-up stated that it had been purchased from a Didcot driver by Frank Burridge for his Bournemouth Museum. He had then sold it on in 1987, and when presented for auction in 2012 it was sold for £22,500.

My Dad, Christopher Kelly, wearing his ABA Referees & Judges Association badge.

The boxing club

Back in 1956 my Dad, Christopher Kelly, ran a boxing club for Didcot boys to get them off the streets and take an interest in something positive until their careers started.

I was 12 years old and was at St Birinus Secondary Modern School for Boys, and my Dad was working on the railway on the coal stage at the time when he was invited to go to Slough and Maidenhead on a Wednesday night to be a boxing referee. Whenever he was not on shiftwork we would travel together by train on one of the free passes that the railway shed master issued; one week we would travel early evening at 5.00pm to Maidenhead, the following week Slough, not getting home till 10.30 at night.

As well as being a referee and boxing judge, Dad also a trainer. He had loved boxing since he had been in the Irish Army. He left school at the age of 14 and, as he said, 'I was thrown into the Irish Army as a boy soldier' by his mother and father as they got the 'silver shilling' and went down the pub to get drunk together. As time moved on Dad became a musician in No 1 Irish Army Band, first playing the clarinet then the violin, becoming proficient in both. He loved sport and was a good sprinter, but boxing was his main sport and he represented the Irish Army at many shows as a lightweight fighter, winning the Leinster Championships. He was also a member of the Arbour Hill Boxing Club in Dublin and boxed for them as well as the Army.

He was selected to box for Ireland in the Golden Gloves Championships in Glasgow, and went into the ring to face his opponent, a black boxer from Chicago. When the bell sounded to finish the first round, Dad turned around to walk back to his corner and his big opponent rabbit-punched him on the back of his neck and broke it. He was sent to a special hospital, but luckily his spinal cord was not badly damaged; nonetheless, he was paralysed and in hospital for two years, lying on his stomach and under treatment till his neck got stronger and better. He never fully regained the feeling in his fingertips so had to give up his instruments and was discharged from the Army on medical grounds.

Dad joined the railway at Didcot shed in 1946. Ten years later someone that Dad knew wrote to us where we lived in Sinodun Road, having discovered that there was a railway boxing championship for railway employees. So Dad approached the railway to organise boxing matches with other depots on the Western Region. He and his two sons, my brothers Paul and Richard (Dick), found the disused building at the back of the Polar Star hostel and rebuilt the room from scratch.

They built a boxing ring and put in boxing items such as a punch bag and ball,

securing them firmly so that they never came away from the ceiling or walls. They cleared the floor and padded it with wooden planks, put in small benches to put clothes on, and secured the main door with heavy locks to stop anyone trying to enter. Electric lights were fitted in the ceiling; some of the expense was met by the railway, while the rest was raised from men Dad had done favours for and those that helped. It looked nothing from the outside, but inside it was a different matter, and looked just like a boxing gym.

Lewis Holmar recalls the precious times he enjoyed with my Dad, especially in the boxing gym. 'He really sharpened me up and the railway staff were simply the best.'

Word got around Didcot that there was a boxing club down at the railway hostel and we saw many boys coming in from St Birinus School. Some older boys really wanted to train and defend themselves against bullies, while others wanted to be taken on as serious boxers and train every week until they were ready to have their first fight. Dad taught them how to stand in the ring and put up their arms and fists to protect their faces, and he went in the ring with them in the gym.

Then he received notification of the first fight at Reading Town Hall for the Western Region Championships. Dick was a light welterweight and entered the match, together with a Welshman from Didcot (whose name I have forgotten) and a couple of the boys who were ready to apply. Dad said it would give them heart.

Dick won two bouts and got into the semi-finals but lost on points. However, it was a good bout. The Welshman also failed to win, and of the other boys that turned up from the club one won and the rest lost. But they derived great interest from sitting at the ringside watching the fights and, as I found every time I went to the events with Dad the excitement was infectious, and it gave them more confidence for next time.

Paul was a bantamweight, small and fiery, and started to train with Dad in the ring. The gym started to take off, and although some went others came in their place. The local paper, *The Didcot Advertiser*, got involved and Dad had some good write-ups about what he had done for the railway. Paul entered for the next match at Swindon and lost, but it was his first bout. Between them my brothers kept it up and won various bouts.

Dad was notified of a return match for the Swindon event, but he did not have anywhere in Didcot big enough to take the amount of people that would come and watch. However, the Army stepped in and said that they would make available a building at Vauxhall Barrack Hall on the Ministry's grounds, and that High-Ranking Officers would like to attend the match. They would put the boxing ring in place and sort out everything. Dad was over the moon!

I was still at school, and the bout was to take place on a Friday night. I noticed two men walking in through the door with women by their sides mouthing off about the place, and really disgracing themselves. All the boxers for the home team were in getting changed, as were the away team. Then one of the Top-Ranking Officers stood in the ring as the Master of Ceremonies, and gave a speech about the Army, the Didcot Railway Boxing Club and the programme. Dad let the Army be the judges and referees as he wanted to watch the matches.

In the first bout, when the bell rang out came the Swindon man and Didcot's Paul Kelly. It took Paul just 60 seconds to knock his opponent clean out and lay him on the canvas stone cold. The Army referee sent Paul back to his corner, Dick laughed, Dad stood amazed, and everyone in the room cheered, clapped and roared. The referee shouted and waved his arms – a knock-out. Paul climbed out of the ring, and the other boxer's wife hit him over the head with her handbag and chased him into the changing room, shouting and screaming at him!

Paul challenged Dick to do the same, so for the second bout Dick got between the ropes and into the ring and warmed up. He was called to the centre of the ring to shake hands with the Swindon boxer, but got a lot of mouth from him. It took Dick three rounds, but he won the match on points. My two brothers were champions, and some of the other young fighters also did well with wins, Lewis Holmar taking home a boxing trophy.

Chapter 7
Ahead Danger – again: 11 September 1952

Appleford Crossing was the scene of another accident ten years later in the early hours of 11 September 1952. This time 'Mogul' No 7311 ran through the sand drag at the end of the loop. The accident occurred a little after 2.00am on a very dark night with no moon. Appleford was on the line between Birmingham and London, and Up and Down Goods Loops started there on either side of the main line. As on the previous occasion, a mixed goods train travelled through the Down Goods Loop at a greater speed than the regulation 10mph, and overran the catch points. The engine was from Reading shed, and is thought to have been travelling at speed to race the fast goods train that was passing at that precise moment.

The Worcester fast goods train that had left Paddington that evening was

2-6-0 No 7311 comes to grief at Appleford Crossing on 11 September 1952. *Great Western Trust collection*

passing on the main line. The crash pulled the rails to one side, and the crew on the engine of the Worcester goods soon realised that something had happened further back down the track; they would have felt it on the footplate with the shuddering of the wagons, then seeing the vacuum gauge needle on the footplate shudder and drop.

The signalman, Gordon Churchman, had a miraculous escape as the goods wagons from the train crashed into the signal box and smashed it to the ground, with its lever frame and instruments spread around. Flung bodily from the signal box into the open, Mr Churchman only suffered light injuries, with bruises to his face, legs and arms. He staggered to the cottage of his shift partner who worked days, Cyril Butterworth, in the village of Appleford, who was in bed but had been awakened by the crash. After helping Mr Churchman to his home in shock, Mr Butterworth raced on his bicycle at great

speed in the darkness along the side of the track, then across the lines to Didcot station, carrying his bike on his shoulder. He raised the alarm at the Telegraph Office, staffed by Jim Hoad, and told him to stop trains coming into the section and the triangle of lines at Didcot. Everybody took great pride in their jobs and knew how to make a sometimes difficult situation easier.

The mixed train was smashed to pieces with wreckage strewn across the crossing gates and signal box. The 'Mogul' was broken in half and had dug into the sand, leaning on her side. Twenty-five wagons had been derailed, the signal box damaged and the signalman injured; however, the drivers escaped injury. The fireman of the goods train ran in the opposite direction waving a red lamp and laid detonators on the Up Main line, in time to stop a light engine travelling south from Hinksey Marshalling yard at Oxford.

The breakdown train was summoned from Didcot shed. Once again the call boys

Above: Another view of No 7311. *Harold Gasson collection*

Below: The signal frame amidst the wreckage of the signal box, but still intact. *Harold Gasson collection*

went out to get the fitters and mates of the breakdown crews back to the shed as quickly as possible. The engine pulled the breakdown train up level with the coal stage so the men could get aboard the coach. As soon as they left the shed area the East signal box gave the 'right away'. Oxford and Worcester trains were being diverted through Princes Risborough, while buses were arranged to pick up passengers at Didcot station who held tickets for local stations between Didcot and Oxford.

Appleford Crossing signal box was totally demolished, and when the dust settled little was left standing, just

Above: This view shows how the box vans demolished the signal box. *Harold Gasson collection*

Right: Appleford Crossing Signal Box in course of reconstruction after the accident. *British Railways*

the damp-course of bricks; everything had fallen inwards, with one of the wagons crashing over on top and leaning on what was left of the box.

Gordon Churchman, the signalman, put in a claim to British Railways for a new motorbike; he rode it from his home in Kynaston Road in Didcot to Appleford for his nightshift. He had stored the bike at the back of the signal box under a shelter he had made. However, the request was refused, as BR said he should not have had it on site near the signal box.

The engineers were soon at work, and in just four weeks the signal box was rebuilt. As before the nameboard was one of the few items that it was possible to salvage from the wrecked box.